MW00575056

ONE THOUSAND SUNS

KRISHNAMURTI AT EIGHTY-FIVE

AND

THE LAST WALK

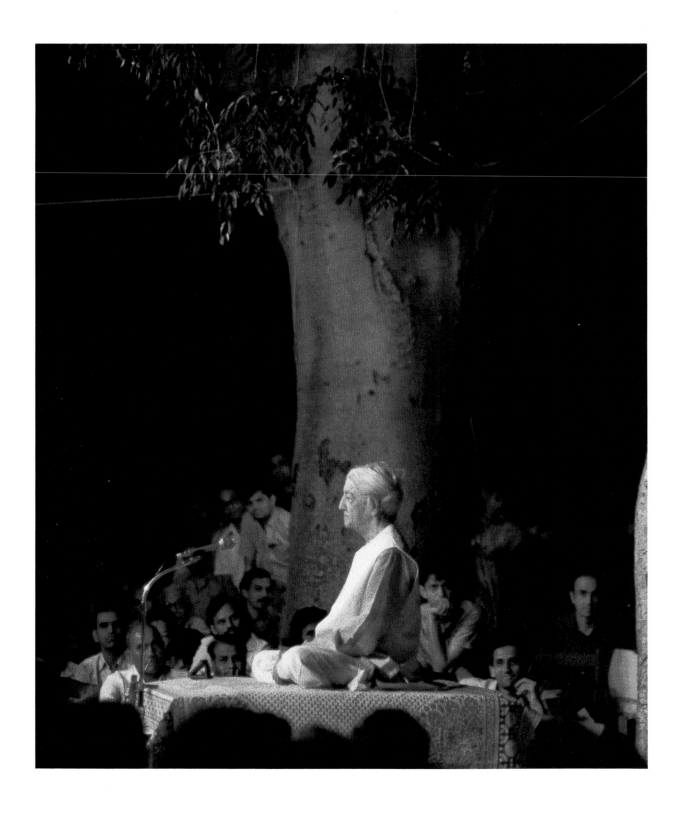

If the splendor of a thousand suns were to appear in the sky,

it would be like the light of the Teachings.

BHAGAVAD GITA, CHAPTER 11, VERSE 12

ONE THOUSAND SUNS

KRISHNAMURTI AT EIGHTY-FIVE

AND

THE LAST WALK

Text and photographs by Asit Chandmal

A P E R T U R E

AUTHOR'S NOTE

It is almost a decade since Krishnamurti died. For years after his death, I found it virtually impossible to read his books, look at the video recordings of his talks, or even speak about the man and his teachings. For the first time in my adult life I refused to take a full-time job, preferring to wander the world and work just enough to earn a decent living and pay for my daughters' education at good schools and universities. They encouraged me in my new mode of life. As my younger daughter Sonali said, "Security can always be recovered, but time can never be returned."

All of us need allies in living. I've seached for ten years for someone to talk to. Finally, I came across a verse by Chuang Tsu:

> The purpose of a fish trap is to catch fish
> and when the fish are caught, the trap is forgotten,
> The purpose of words is to convey ideas,
> and when the ideas are grasped, the words are
> forgotten,
> Where can I find a man who has forgotten words?
> He is the one I would like to talk to.

Nowadays, the only human beings I can take my problems to, and have long meaningful conversations with, are my daughters Clea and Sonali. And yet, clearly, there are some things that we cannot communicate with one another. The difference of thirty years cannot be wished away. On such occasions, I miss Krishnamurti terribly.

In this book, I have made no attempt either to summarize or to expound Krishnamurti's teachings; for that, one must go to his words, to his books. However, I have included in my memoirs of Krishnamurti incidents and conversations that I believe convey something worth preserving: how Krishnamurti talks to and counsels a child, a young man, and a middle-aged worldly adult. At every age, whenever I had a problem, I went to Krishnamurti. I received great affection and advice that solved my problem for at least a short time. Much had to be left out; one has to read between the lines. In some places throughout the text, I have referred to Krishnamurti as "Krishnaji" (the suffix *ji* denotes respect)—this was a name people called him in India.

I am most grateful to Michael Hoffman for his practical and quick decision making on a number of issues, and to Diana Stoll's painstaking and perceptive editing of the new material in this book. Without their unstinting help and encouragement, this new edition would not have been possible. My thanks are also extended to Mary Cadogan for giving me permission to reproduce "The Core of Krishnamurti's Teachings."

— A. C.

One Thousand Suns was originally published in 1985 by Harry N. Abrams as *One Thousand Moons*.

Library of Congress Catalog Card Number: 95-75433

Hardcover ISBN: 0-89381-631-0
Composition by Susi Oberhelman,
based on the original design by Tina Davis
Printed and bound by Everbest, Hong Kong

The Staff at Aperture for *One Thousand Suns* is:
Michael E. Hoffman, Executive Director
Allegra C. D'Adamo, Associate Publisher
Diana C. Stoll, Editor
Michael Sand, Managing Editor
Stevan A. Baron, Production Director
Sandra Greve, Production Manager
Michael Lorenzini, Editorial Assistant
Marcy Gerstein, Editorial Work-Scholar
Laurie Burgan, Production Work-Scholar

Aperture Foundation publishes a periodical, books, and portfolios of fine photography to communicate with serious photographers and creative people everywhere. A complete catalog is available upon request. Address: 20 East 23rd Street, New York, New York 10010. Phone: (212) 598-4205. Fax: (212) 598-4015.

Information about Krishnamurti's publications and recordings can be obtained from the following institutions:

Krishnamurti Foundation Trust
Brockwood Park
Bramdean, Hants., SO24 OLQ
UNITED KINGDOM

Krishnamurti Foundation America
P.O. Box 1560
Ojai, CA, 93024-1560
U.S.A.

Krishnamurti Foundation India
Vasant Vihar 64/65 Greenways Road
Madras 600 028
INDIA

FIRST EDITION

10 9 8 7 6 5 4 3 2 1

CONTENTS

Krishnamurti, 1934. Photo by Edward Weston.

PREFACE

The idea for this book came while I was with Krishnamurti in Madras in January 1980. It occurred to me that there was no dichotomy between his life and his teachings. The teachings were intellectual, logical, and rigorous. His daily life and conversations were simple. He was an ordinary human being in private life, yet the other Krishnamurti, the teacher, was clearly of extraordinary energy, intelligence and insight. The man on the public platform and the man away from it were different, but there was no contradiction between what he said and what he did.

I used to wonder why the words of a Buddha or a Christ or a Mohammed could still capture the minds and hearts of more than half of humanity. These were simple men, who lived millennia ago, and yet their powerful hold on so many people was beyond all understanding when one considered the thinkers who had preceded and followed them. What did these men have or do that others did not?

And so I turned to Krishnamurti. His life was a legend. I knew him well. If I could spend time traveling with him, being with him, photographing him, observing how he actually lived, then perhaps I could find an answer. I asked Krishnamurti if I could do a book on him. He agreed readily. He said I could do what I wanted, take photographs at any time, in any situation, and write about whatever I saw and felt.

And so the book began, with the first tentative, hesitant photographs. As I traveled with him, and watched him, I found that there was nothing he forbade me. I took pictures, I started writing. And then a strange thing happened. Instead of his life unfolding, I found that the more I probed the more I came face to face with myself. As I explored his life, his quotidian activities, I began to confront myself more and more, to reexamine everything about my own daily life. In the beginning it was effortless; there was a recollection of my conversations with him at various times since I was nine years old. Later it became more difficult, as if I wanted to erase the responses excavated by his questions.

So what began as a journey into another man's life ended with an unfinished journey into mine.

I did not find the answer to my original question. Perhaps the immense energy that comes into being when there is no conflict between what you think, what you say, and what you do, results in direct communication, which is independent of time, and therefore exists for many generations.

This book was conceived and created in Krishnaji's eighty-fifth year; he had lived for a thousand months or a thousand moons, hence the book's original title, *One Thousand Moons*.

The book is dedicated to my grandmother, Iravati Mehta, or Moti Mama as we all called her. My grandmother told me when I was nine, "It is more important to be with Krishnaji than to go to school," and she acted accordingly and took me with her to Poona to stay with Krishnaji. I did not have the same insight or courage when it came to my own children, Clea and Sonali, but in the making of this book, falteringly, hesitantly, I started moving toward the same conclusion.

My aunts, Pupul Jayakar, the most intelligent, and Nandini Mehta, the most beautiful, had their lives altered totally, but in different ways, by their meetings with Krishnaji. They have their own stories to tell, and they are told in Pupul Jayakar's book on Krishnaji. The chapter in this book on his daily life at eighty-five was extracted, with modifications, from the draft manuscript of Pupul Jayakar's book.

A great many people assisted in the compilation of this book. Mary Zimbalist was supportive and instructive from the start. Mary Lutyens and Mary Cadogan offered the help I asked for. Tina Davis worked heroically to sort through almost fifteen hundred photographs, all uncaptioned; she was in New York, and I in either Asia or Europe. We met once in New York to finalize the layouts and she had done an excellent job in decoding the photos and instinctively recognizing the documentary importance of some of them. Incidentally all photographs were taken in available light and not one was arranged or posed. The idea was to document and record, not to take beautiful pictures. Charan and Nimisha Sharma, and my wife, Minakshi, did the first layout and dummy. These fifteen hundred photographs of Krishnaji are like family snapshots to me—I find every one of them worth keeping and impossible to discard. Without Nimisha, Charan, Minakshi, and Tina, the photographs would have remained unsorted and unedited.

This book owes its existence to M, who helped so much.

—ASIT CHANDMAL

J. Krishnamurti

Krishnamurti in Adyar, 1910.

KRISHNAMURTI: HIS EARLY LIFE

Madanapalle is a small town in the heart of South India. It is in the Chittoor District of Andhra Pradesh, about 150 miles from Madras.

A century ago a young Brahmin named Jiddu Narianiah moved to Madanapalle with his wife, Jiddu Sanjeevamma, who was also his second cousin. (The family name, Jiddu, came from their ancestral village.)

Like others of his caste, Narianiah had a puja room in his home. Puja is prayer. An orthodox Brahmin woman does not enter the puja room or a temple while giving birth. It is sacrilegious.

Sanjeevamma insisted on giving birth to her eighth child in the puja room.

The child was born half an hour after midnight on May 11, 1895, or 12:30 A.M. on May 12. He was named Krishnamurti, after Lord Krishna, who was also the eighth born according to Hindu mythology.

It is recorded that Krishnamurti's horoscope was cast by the local astrologer, who predicted religious greatness and global fame for the infant.

Until he was almost fifteen, nothing in the boy's life gave any indication that he would be famous; nothing in his behavior for the next twenty years, till he was almost thirty-five, gave any indication that he would be a great religious teacher. And yet this was the man about whom the greatest skeptics in the world, who were also the most articulate of men, wrote in terms that had the dimension of hyperbole.

George Bernard Shaw called Krishnamurti "a religious figure of the greatest distinction," and added, "He is the most beautiful human being I have ever seen."

Henry Miller wrote, "There is no man I would consider it a greater privilege to meet...."

Aldous Huxley, after attending one of Krishnamurti's lectures, confided in a letter "...the most impressive thing I have listened to. It was like listening to a discourse of the Buddha—such power, such intrinsic authority...."

Kahlil Gibran wrote, "When he entered my room I said to myself, 'Surely the Lord of Love has come.'"

•

Krishnamurti, at ninety, is still very much alive. He travels the world, addresses thousands in the United States, Asia, and Europe; is interviewed, televised, published, feted, adored, worshiped, and criticized; and yet his life is an enigma. While every detail of his early years has been meticulously recorded, it is full of myth, magic, and mystery. When you meet Krishnamurti, and are mesmerized by his magic, your modern mind starts believing the legends of his youth. The mystery, however, remains.

Krishnamurti hides nothing. He has seminars and dialogues with world-famous scientists, writers, psychiatrists, artists, sociologists, Buddhist scholars, politicians and prime ministers, and yet the mystery remains.

And so instead of attempting to interpret or understand or explain his life, one can merely repeat what others have witnessed and recorded.

•

The story begins even earlier than 1895. The Theosophical Society was founded in 1875 in New York City by Madame Helena Petrovna Blavatsky, née Von Hahn. She was of Russian origin and had based the principles of the Society on many esoteric and occult teachings—the Kabala, Gnosticism, Meister Eckhart, Paracelsus, and later, Hindu, Buddhist, and Tibetan beliefs such as karma and reincarnation.

However, two central beliefs are important and relevant to any retelling of the life of Krishnamurti. The first, that there are Masters, or Adepts, who are perfected human beings and who guide the spiritual evolution of Man. Some of these Masters live in the Himalayas and can be contacted on the astral plane by those who have the occult powers to do so.

The second belief is that Lord Maitreya (who in the Theosophical hierarchy is even higher than the Masters but lower than the Buddha) would again reincarnate himself in a human body, as he had done in the body of Jesus.

The coming of the World Teacher was therefore central to Theosophy; it would happen when Lord Maitreya found the right body, the right vehicle, to incarnate in, and the body, the being, would be prepared and protected by the Masters. None of this, by itself, would be astonishing. However, Madame Blavatsky, and later Dr. Annie Besant, actually set up a worldwide organization to prepare for the coming of the World Teacher.

One of the organization's purposes was to "find" a person, somewhere on earth, whose being and body were such that the Lord Maitreya himself could incarnate in the found vehicle. And the only thing the leaders of the Society had to go on was their faith in their own occult powers.

Annie Besant, née Wood, was born in 1847 in London. She

read Madame Blavatsky's book *The Secret Doctrine* when she was about forty. She was immediately converted. She met Blavatsky in 1888 and joined the Theosophical Society in 1889.

Annie Besant would have been considered a remarkable woman in any society, in any era. She separated from her husband when she was twenty-six and plunged into the most modern causes and movements. She was a close associate of Charles Bradlaugh, a great public figure and atheist; she advocated birth control publicly and vigorously; she became a prominent Fabian, counting George Bernard Shaw and Sidney and Beatrice Webb among her close friends and colleagues; she was president of the Theosophical Society from 1907 until her death in 1933; and in 1916 she founded the Indian Home Rule League, striving with figures such as Mahatma Gandhi for Indian independence; and she was considered one of the greatest orators of her time.

It was she who would "adopt" the boy Krishnamurti, proclaim him the coming Messiah, the World Teacher to be, set up an enormous global organization with large funds and thousands of followers to provide the infrastructure for Krishnamurti's teachings, take great personal interest in his upbringing and education (Krishnamurti always called her Amma or Mother), and remain utterly loyal to Krishnamurti even when he rejected the great organization she had built for him.

But Krishnamurti was "found" by another man—Charles Webster Leadbeater, who had journeyed in 1884 with Blavatsky to India, to Adyar, Madras, where she had set up the Theosophical Society headquarters. Leadbeater was a powerful figure, resembling George Bernard Shaw, and he claimed to have developed occult powers, including the ability to see and interpret the aura surrounding each human being; he also claimed to be able to communicate with the Masters.

Narianiah retired and moved to Adyar in January 1909. Krishnamurti's mother had died four years earlier, and Narianiah's family consisted of his four surviving sons.

Krishnamurti was the second eldest of the four and had spent his childhood as a dreamy and vague boy not interested in school or learning, but fascinated by nature and mechanical things. He would watch ants for hours or take apart his father's watch to see how it worked. He was attached to his mother and to his younger brother, Nitya, but evidently to nothing else, especially not to any material things. He was regularly punished at school, but it did not seem to have any effect on him. This was a quality that he retained throughout his life: neither praise nor criticism left a mark on him. Equally, no one else's thoughts or ideas ever influenced him, a quality that stood him in good stead when he was being brought up and educated by Theosophists in the East and the West. Krishnamurti once described this as being like a vessel with many holes: whatever is poured in goes out, nothing remains.

It was 1909, and Krishnamurti was fourteen years old. He was playing and bathing on the beach at Adyar. Leadbeater saw

Krishnamurti's aura and found it wonderful, with not a particle of selfishness in it. It was suggested to Narianiah that the Theosophical Society would bring up Krishnamurti and his younger brother, Nitya. And so began the grooming of the World Teacher. The discovery of Krishnamurti is inexplicable unless you are a believer in Leadbeater's occult powers.

Krishnamurti was "instructed" by the Masters, especially Master Kuthumi, who was fair, with blue eyes, brown hair and beard, and lived somewhere in Tibet in the body of his last incarnation, that of a Kashmiri Brahmin. With the help of Leadbeater, Krishnamurti would visit the Master Kuthumi on the astral plane at night and write down his teachings in the morning. His writings were eventually published in 1910, when Krishnamurti was fifteen. Titled *At the Feet of the Master*, it has been translated into almost thirty languages, and it is still in print. During the day Leadbeater and his close associates gave Krishnamurti a more conventional education. They taught him English, not only the language but the modes of behavior.

The boy had undoubted psychic powers that were revealed when they tested him. He could easily read unopened letters and people's thoughts.

In 1911, Annie Besant took Krishnamurti and his brother Nitya to England. They returned to India for a short visit and in 1912 went back to England. They were to stay in Europe for ten years before seeing India again.

The boys were brought up in aristocratic upper-class English society, primarily by Lady Emily Lutyens, the daughter of a viceroy of India and the wife of Sir Edwin Lutyens, the architect of New Delhi. They did all the normal things for boys of their age and situation in society—had private tutors, dressed immaculately, cultivated beautiful manners, spoke English and French perfectly, went to the theater, played golf, and vacationed on the Continent. Slowly every vestige of his Hindu boyhood was removed from Krishnamurti.

Krishnamurti proceeded to fail every single examination he sat for. He was refused admission to Oxford despite his connections (one of them purportedly being the son of God), and he could not complete his studies at London University or at the Sorbonne.

Krishnamurti was probably an unhappy, agitated, and lonely boy, who seems to have undergone some of the afflictions of adolescence. Mrs. Besant was too busy fighting for freedom in India, and Krishnamurti and Nitya were virtually living in exile during the First World War in an alien country. Krishnamurti was constantly being reminded that he had a great future, great responsibilities, for he would be the World Teacher, and thousands in many countries were donating money and devoting their lives to building an organization for him and his teachings, and many more thousands were eagerly awaiting the day when he would appear before them and propound the Teachings.

One of the tangibles in Krishnamurti's life is that none of this seems to have had any effect on him inwardly. Outwardly, he was, and remained, a shy, considerate, and gentle person;

however he seems to have been vague and even frivolous in those days, qualities difficult to imagine for anyone who has come across him in the last fifty years. Mrs. Besant, Leadbeater, and the Theosophists really protected Krishnamurti. Nobody could touch him or, even, his tennis racket. As far as possible he had two companions, and even the adjoining compartments of the train in which he traveled were occupied by his protectors.

His brother Nitya had been given the same upbringing, but he did not have to become the World Teacher. Nitya and Krishnamurti were devoted to each other. Nitya was bright and passed his exams easily. He wanted to make money, marry, and live a normal life. All this was denied to him. He was to protect and look after Krishnamurti. Nitya was never very healthy physically and was to contract tuberculosis.

It was suggested to Krishnamurti that the climate at Ojai, a valley inland from Santa Barbara, California, would be ideal for Nitya. The American Indians called the valley Ojai, or the nest, and it is covered with groves of orange trees. Krishnamurti and Nitya went to Ojai and stayed in a place called Pine Cottage.

It was here, in August 1922, that a strange "process" began, the first external evidence that something inexplicable and mystical was happening to Krishnamurti. There were several eye-witnesses, and Nitya wrote an account of the process for Mrs. Besant and Charles Leadbeater. Krishnamurti too wrote about his experiences.

For three days, from August 17 through August 20, Krishnamurti's body was racked with pain. He was unconscious a great deal of the time, cried out, could not bear to be touched, complained of dirty surroundings and pain in his head and neck, fainted, did not eat, shivered and yet complained of heat, was in agony most of the time and strangely quiet for some of the time, and then on the third day he sat under a young pepper tree and started chanting. The Buddha, Lord Maitreya, and other celestial beings seem to have appeared before Krishnamurti, and he went into a deep trance. Krishnamurti's account of this experience ends with the words "I am God intoxicated."

Neither Annie Besant nor Charles Leadbeater could fully explain this process, which Krishnamurti was to undergo with some variations at different times for many years.

One explanation was that his brain and body were being purified to the nth degree so that the Lord Maitreya could inhabit the vehicle. Another explanation is that it was the rising of the Kundalini in Krishnamurti's body; the Kundalini and its awakening, from the base of the spine, upward along the spine and neck to the centers of the brain and the opening of the third eye, has been described for millennia by Hindu sages. The descriptions are uncannily similar to Krishnamurti's experiences.

Krishnamurti has no memory now of his experiences of the

Krishnamurti with Nitya, 1910.

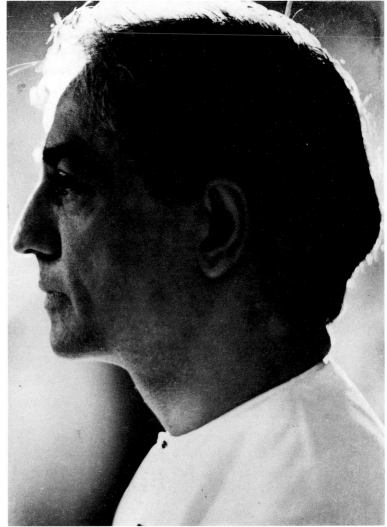

Krishnamurti in India, 1948.

process. Knowing the absolute integrity and total lack of superstitious mumbo jumbo in Krishnamurti, one can only state that something vitally important and completely inexplicable happened to Krishnamurti in August 1922, when he was twenty-seven years old.

Outwardly his life did not change. He continued to travel, to give talks organized under the auspices of the Theosophical Society, and the Order of the Star of the East, which had been created for him. And he did not say anything startling or different. He seemed a follower, a person being prepared to be a vehicle for the World Teacher.

In 1923 Annie Besant bought Pine Cottage and six acres in Ojai for Krishnamurti and Nitya; the land had a larger house that was renamed Arya Vihar and was next to Pine Cottage and the pepper tree. Several hundred acres of land were later bought for future use, for starting schools.

Baron von Pallandt offered Castle Eerde, in Ommen, Holland, with five thousand acres of land to Krishnamurti; this was used to hold annual "camps" or conventions.

And then the great turning point in Krishnamurti's life occurred in November 1925.

Krishnamurti and Nitya were at Ojai, and Nitya had not been well. Krishnamurti was asked to travel to India to give talks organized by the Theosophical Society. He did not want to leave Nitya alone. However he was assured by the leaders of the Society that the Masters would protect Nitya. Nitya would not be allowed to die.

Reluctantly Krishnamurti left for India. When his ship was in the Suez Canal he received a telegram: Nitya had died.

Krishnamurti was stunned. According to eyewitnesses, who were also close associates, Krishnamurti wept for several days and nights. However he stayed with his sorrow, making no attempt at escape or explanation, and by the time the ship reached India, the crisis had passed.

But Krishnamurti was never to depend on anything or be attached to anyone again, and this became a central theme in his teachings.

From 1926 to 1929 Krishnamurti continued traveling to India, Europe, and America. However a change had clearly taken place, evident from his pronouncements at various public gatherings. He had become more thoughtful, more serious, less willing to be told what to do.

The great break with the Theosophical Society came in August 1929. At the Ommen Camp in Holland, in front of Mrs. Besant and an audience of more than three thousand members, Krishnamurti dissolved the Order of the Star. Among other things, he said that Truth was a pathless land, and no organization should be formed to lead or coerce people along any particular path, because Truth, being limitless and unconditional, could not be organized and was unapproachable through any religion, sect, or organization.

He said he did not want to belong to any organization of a spiritual kind, because such an organization becomes a crutch, a weakness, a bondage, and cripples the individual.

He said that he did not want any followers or disciples, because the moment you follow someone you cease to follow Truth.

He said that no one holds the key to Truth, that key is your own self, and in the purification and incorruptibility of that self alone...

He said that he had contemplated the situation for over two years, slowly, carefully, and patiently; that he had not been persuaded by anyone ("I am not persuaded in such things") and that his decision was final.

It was a great shock to everyone. Krishnamurti resigned from the Theosophical Society and from every organization, Order, and Trust of which he was a member. He gave up everything that had been given to him.

He was thirty-four years old.

Krishnamurti had never had any desire for money, power, or a comfortable life. When people told him that his was a magnificent act of renunciation and asked him what he would now do, Krishnamurti replied that his only concern was to set man free, to free man from all cages, from all fears; he would not found a new religion nor establish new theories or philosophies. Instead he would go around the world, meeting and talking to people, because "if there are only five people who will listen, who will live, who have their faces turned to eternity, it will be sufficient."

Annie Besant remained loyal to him. She died in 1933, at eighty-six, and Charles Leadbeater died in 1934 at the age of eighty-seven.

Krishnamurti spent the years of the Second World War at Ojai. It was during those years that he met and befriended Aldous Huxley and other intellectuals. He moved equally easily with their friends from Hollywood, among whom were Greta Garbo, Charlie Chaplin, and John Barrymore. (He turned down the latter's offer to act as the Buddha in a film. He was to be paid five thousand dollars a week.)

He went to India in 1948, a time of great upheaval. India had just become independent, and when Mahatma Gandhi was assassinated, it has been written that "it was to Krishnamurti that Jawaharlal Nehru brought, in secret, his solitary anguish."

Huxley encouraged Krishnamurti to write and to publish. *Education and the Significance of Life* (1953), *The First and Last Freedom* (1954), and *Commentaries on Living* (1956) became the first of over thirty books published through the years in the United States, Europe, and India. They are written in his own words, and together with his public talks—many of which are available on videocassettes—they contain his teachings as they unfolded in the last four decades.

It is impossible to summarize Krishnamurti's teachings. I am convinced that the printed words by themselves do not convey as much as the public talks do, and that the public talks take on much greater meaning when one sees the teachings personified in the daily life of Krishnamurti.

KRISHNAMURTI'S LIFE AT AGE EIGHTY-FIVE

Krishnaji wakes at sunrise, and lies in bed, every sense alert. Not a single thought arises, and then there is a coming to, from vast distances.

He starts the morning with forty-five minutes of yogic asanas and thirty-five minutes of pranayam, or breathing exercises.

At about eight, Krishnaji has breakfast, which consists of fruit; cereal such as muesli; yogurt; nuts; eggs; toast; and butter— never tea or coffee. His breakfast in India sometimes includes South Indian idlis or dosas instead of cereal. He drinks a tablespoon of the green juice of a bitter gourd.

In the West he breakfasts alone and quietly. In India, however, his close associates gather. Over breakfast there is discussion on education and the schools, on consciousness, the seed of disintegration in man, computers and artificial intelligence, the possible mutation of the human mind, on death, the nature of God, and so on.

The conversation moves to international affairs, scientific discoveries, war and nuclear disarmament. Krishnaji has an intense curiosity and questions deeply. New discoveries in science and new technological advances fascinate him.

He asks for news of what is happening in the world. The state of the country is freely discussed; the violence, corruption, the decay of values; every problem is raised and probed.

Everyone participates, and there is no sense of the teacher and the taught.

There are questions he often asks: What is happening in the country? Why has it lost all creativity? Why is there degeneration? No one answer satisfies him. It is as if the serious individual has to hold these questions within him to awaken to their intimations. The questions have to be asked and the mind remain with them, ponder them. Krishnaji's span of attention is formidable. He once said that some questions have to be held in the mind for eternity.

When he is to hold his morning dialogues, the breakfast session is shorter. A small group that is to participate in the discussions gathers at ten and the discussions continue until eleven-thirty. When there are no organized group discussions, his talks with his associates continue at the breakfast table for two or three hours. Some of his most intense insights have been revealed at these sessions. He often refers to himself in the third person—as "K"—during these conversations.

By eleven-thirty he goes to his room and lies down for half an hour with the *Economist, Time,* or *Newsweek;* or picture books of trees, mountains, birds, and animals; or detective and mystery novels. He never reads serious books, but is very well informed on the state of the world.

At midday, he has an oil massage, a very hot bath, and lunch is at one-fifteen.

Krishnaji eats very slowly; his associates finish eating long before he does. He tastes and chews everything very carefully and savors and comments on the food when it's excellent. Lunch usually lasts over two hours.

In India he eats Indian food, though he always starts with fruit and salad. He rarely eats fried or sweet food. He likes hot pickles and permits himself tiny portions of them. Again at lunchtime there is discussion. In the West he first eats fruit and salads, in that order, then soup, followed by a cooked dish, which could be Italian, French, Mexican, or English. It is at lunch that discussions with his friends and associates take place in the West. Krishnaji sometimes tells stories, talks about his encounters with wild animals, or jokes about St. Peter, heaven and hell, as well as stories of Russia and the commissars. He intersperses these with serious talk.

In the West Krishnaji helps to clear the table, wash the dishes, and clean the kitchen. In India, the servants take care of that. After lunch he returns to his room and takes a nap. At about four o'clock, he sees a few people: a woman going blind or a mother grieving over the death of her child.

With the sun about to set, he goes for a walk. His strides are long, his body erect. His friends walk with him. He walks briskly for five kilometers, watching, listening, smelling the earth. He picks up and throws aside stones lying on the path. There is very little conversation. He has said that not a single thought touches his mind during these walks.

He hardly ever misses his walk, regardless of the weather or how he is feeling. On a long flight I have seen him walk up and down the aisle of the plane.

Returning home, he washes, then once again does some breathing exercises. He eats a light supper—the food is the same as at lunch. On some occasions, with a few friends, he sits over the dinner table and hints of an eternity that lies beyond the mind. In the West, he eats alone in bed, his food on a tray, while watching television or reading a book.

When he is not feeling well, or to keep himself physically healthy, he tries all kinds of herbal and ayurvedic remedies. He regularly takes vitamin and mineral tablets with breakfast. He experiments with his diet; at times he has gone on a protein diet; at times he has drunk a sip of milk and orange juice alternately; at other times he has given up all milk and lived on raw foods. For the past twenty years he has insisted on eating fruit first, then raw salads, and only then cooked food, with a little dessert at the end. He does not drink wine or any other alcoholic beverage and has never smoked in his life. He has always been a vegetarian.

He is very particular about his clothes and looks after them carefully. He is always elegantly and appropriately dressed—whether it be jeans, shirt, and jogging shoes in California, or a suit in London, or Indian clothes in India. He likes to polish his own shoes and sometimes those of others.

He occasionally goes to see movies: he likes Westerns. He sometimes visits museums. He watches television very often and listens to classical music, both Western and Indian.

Every year Krishnamurti travels throughout the world talking to individuals, small groups, or addressing thousands of people at public talks. He has been traveling for over sixty years, never staying more than a few weeks in each place. He has traveled and spoken directly to more people than any man in history.

He only goes where he is invited. From mid-February to the end of May, he is in the United States, mainly in Ojai, California, eighty miles north of Los Angeles. He stays at Pine Cottage near Arya Vihar. He has lived there since 1922. He gives several public talks. He makes trips to New York, San Francisco, or, say, Los Alamos, New Mexico, if invited to give talks or hold seminars. There is a Krishnamurti Foundation of America (KFA) school at Ojai where he talks to the parents and staff about education and the significance of life.

He spends June at the KFE school in Brockwood Park, Hampshire, England. The school was founded in 1969 with a large part of the initial money funded by a gift the donor originally intended to give to Krishnamurti for his personal use. At Brockwood he has discussions with the teachers, students, and staff.

He moves to Gstaad, Switzerland, in July. A chalet is rented. Krishnamurti eats at the chalet, occasionally driving to a restaurant for lunch. Krishnamurti holds several question-and-answer sessions, and gives six or seven public talks to about three thousand people who come to hear him every year. He returns to Brockwood Park in the second half of August and stays until the end of October. Again there are several public talks and discussions, as well as private interviews.

Starting in November he spends three and a half months in India. He goes to New Delhi first and then Benares, where he stays on the grounds of the educational institutions founded by him at Rajghat over the last fifty years. He spends about two or three weeks in each place.

He then moves to Madras, where he stays at Vasant Vihar, the headquarters of the KFI. He spends four weeks in Madras, and then three to four weeks at the school in Rishi Valley, a hundred and fifty miles east of Madras, which he founded in 1926.

On his way to Europe and the United States, he spends three weeks in Bombay, and lives in the Sterling Apartments.

At his public talks in India, some of which are attended by about seven thousand people, he still wears a broad red-bordered dhoti and a long honey-toned kurta. In the West, he wears a shirt, slacks, and a cardigan, or a suit if he talks in a city. Krishnamurti walks to the dais surrounded—but untouched—by people. As he sits in silence on the platform, Krishnamurti's presence reaches out and draws his listeners close to him. Then he starts to speak.

The back is erect, the face untouched by time. The voice is clear, strong, probing, unfolding the problem, letting it open and reveal itself, exploring every nuance. His hands rest in his lap, occasionally they move, gesturing eloquently. For over an hour and a half the vast audience sits, silent, with hardly any movement. After the talk is over Krishnamurti sits still.

The thousands in the audience sit or stand motionless as if totally absorbed.

In Switzerland, Krishnamurti walks out of the tent after his talk, onto a path leading toward Saanen. He walks briskly. Men, women, and children come out of the tent and gaze at him, standing still as if mesmerized. After a couple of hundred yards he gets into the car that takes him back to the chalet.

In England, Krishnamurti returns, after changing his clothes, to the tent where lunch is served. Krishnamurti mixes with the audience. Everyone is polite. No one stares at him. Someone comes up and engages him in some inconsequential conversation. Krishnamurti eats standing up or walking around.

In India, he folds his hands in namaste and the crowds surge toward him. He reaches out with both hands and allows them to be held by those that can reach him. Then, slowly, he extricates himself. He gets down from the platform. There is only a tiny passage through this mass of people. They touch their faces to his hands. He does not draw his hands away but keeps them extended. It looks as if a stampede is inevitable, but the silence of his presence creates order. People move back slightly and he walks through.

In Bombay, in the car, when his companions try to close the window, Krishnamurti stops them. His arms reach out through the windows. All the way to the gate, men and women press on the car, touching his hands, putting them to their eyes. Children wait at the Sterling Apartments flat with a garland of jasmine and roses. He takes it with grace, wears it around his neck for some moments, before giving it to a child near him. He does not like people to touch his feet, bending to touch theirs if they attempt to.

As he enters his tenth decade, the urgency has increased, so has the drive. Nothing seems to tire him. He pushes the body, walking faster, testing himself, so that most people half his age cannot keep up with him.

By ten-thirty at night he is asleep. Just before he sleeps the whole day passes swiftly through his mind. In a flash the day and its events are quenched. He rarely dreams. There are no yesterdays.

In 1980, Krishnamurti was to tell my aunt, Pupul Jayakar, that when he stopped speaking, his body would die. The body existed for only one purpose, to reveal the Teaching.

KRISHNAMURTI: A MEMOIR

When I was nine I stayed with Krishnaji in Poona for several weeks. My grandmother had set up house in the Servants of India Society—there were two bedrooms and a living room in between. The dining room and the kitchen were in a separate cottage two hundred yards away.

We used to walk together to the cottage for lunch—his umbrella always protecting him against even a hint of sun.

He often asked me to run to the cottage—he ran with me, and we finished together. I was nine and he was six times my age—fifty-four.

When he saw me flying kites he told me about the enormous kites in California, larger in span than his outstretched arms, and later, when it was Diwali, we went to the markets of Poona, bought firecrackers, and lit them at night. Once, when I shied away from a bursting bomb he said, "Watch it. Don't look away."

•

When I was fourteen, I visited him at Ratansi Morarji's house on Carmichael Road in Bombay.

I asked him, "Should I meditate?"

He said, "No, you are too young. Play with it. Play with everything. Look at girls, flowers. Don't take things seriously. The mind does not mature until it is forty."

The next day I went to see him again at Carmichael Road. We sat quietly. I felt a gradual untangling of myself, and as it evolved, I could sense resistance, reluctance to let go. Pure peace flooded me. (I am trying to revive a memory that has committed suicide.) After a few minutes I left. We had not spoken, not touched.

For many years thereafter he used to touch me on my chest or back, over my heart, lightly, while parting or meeting, and the tension fell away from me like sand in the sun.

•

I met him the same evening at a large dinner party at my aunt's house on Warden Road. He crossed the room, sat beside me, and asked, "What books do you read?"

"Comics and magazines," I replied. He asked me to get a pencil and paper and told me to write down the names of authors: Aldous Huxley, D. H. Lawrence, P. G. Wodehouse, Lewis Mumford, Sinclair Lewis, Emil Ludwig, "especially Napoleon," and Bertrand Russell, among others. He said I should read books written by these writers.

"Have you read them?" I asked.

"No," he replied, "but my brother did."

•

Until I was sixteen I was innocent of sex. After that it became a half-understood ecstasy. I went to see Krishnaji in Benares that winter. I traveled in a third-class train compartment across India with Rao Sahab Patwardhan—it took twenty-four hours, and we shared the compartment with local milkmen, cows, vegetable vendors, and other villagers. Though I stayed in Rajghat, on the banks of the Ganges, where schools and a college had been started decades ago by Krishnaji, and where everyone including Krishnaji stayed, I did not meet him for two days.

And then one evening I saw Krishnaji from a distance on his daily walk. He came up to me, asked how I was, and continued walking. I did not see him again for two days. I was extremely depressed and lonely. I cried alot. Suddenly the desire to understand sex became very strong. The next day I went to talk to Krishnaji about it.

"Thought is the sexual problem," he said. "Listen to desire as you would to a song, or to the breeze amongst the trees."

He said, "Don't let sex precipitate you into marriage. If you marry a girl who is not beautiful you won't be happy. You will play around with others."

"And if I married someone very beautiful?"

"Oh no, that won't make you happy—she will play around."

•

After that, at Rajghat, we went for a walk every day. We walked by the river, the Ganga, and through mango groves. We used to take the old road to Sarnath, and he told me, "The Buddha walked here."

Then he said, "It is very important to do something you really love. I know a man who loves painting, and he paints. His relatives look after him. Once you take a job, or anything like that, then the struggle begins, of wanting a better position, ambition, outdoing your colleagues, competition. It will wear you out, destroy you.

He continued, "Do what you love. You will notice, while playing tennis, that if you play because you enjoy it rather than with the thought of winning, you will play much better.

"I used to be a scratch golfer," he added, "but I could not play if there was a tournament or a wager on the game."

We walked silently for a while, and then he said, "At your age you can do anything you want, in three months, if you set your mind to it."

•

I was sitting with Krishnaji in his room overlooking the river. We sat in silence, and then he said, "I wish you could travel with me, and meet the variety of people I see. Doctors, writers, scientists, artists, so-called religious men, philosophers, wives and mothers and husbands, clerks, bureaucrats, and their bosses…"

"Yes, I'd like to travel with you," I replied.

"One day you will, you will see," he said.

He then asked me, "When you read certain authors, do you feel the urge to write?"

"Yes," I replied.

He suggested that I should write, that it would bring order and clarity. He told me that even when he was ill and tired, he used to write for half an hour every day. Sometimes he used to force himself to do it, though he admitted he should not have done that.

"Writing will help you in everyday life, in mathematics, in conversation. The most important thing is that when you are mature you have the capacity to see a thing to its very end. The mind becomes sharp and clear through writing, discussing."

Then he added, "Write every day. A few pages, get a loose-leaf notebook, but write every day."

He said, "I write between interviews, on planes, a few pages every day. It is part of your life, not separate from it."

And so I started a diary. I quote from the entry dated 20 March 1957: "…somehow, after my talk with Krishnaji in Benares, I am no longer troubled by sexual thoughts."

I was almost eighteen years old.

●

I went to London, to study, at nineteen. The next year Krishnaji came and invited me to Mrs. Bindley's apartment in Kensington. He asked me a great many questions about my London life and then took me upstairs and opened a cupboard. Inside was a row of suits — from Savile Row.

He said, "Take them, take whatever you want."

I took my jacket off, and even I could smell my unbathed body. He tried to help me put on his jackets, but they were too tight, and after some time he said, "No, they won't fit." He gave me his ties and electric shaver and said, "I wish I could take you to Huntsman and outfit you with suits and then to Lobb's for shoes."

He added, "Be scrupulously clean. And you must be well dressed. Always, even at home when you are alone."

●

Fear of madness surfaced and panicked me when I was twenty-two. My father had had fits. He left my mother when I was six or seven, and I didn't see him again till I was nineteen, just before I left for England. He was educated at Balliol College, Oxford, and entered the Indian Civil Service, and then he had given it all up, including a good job in a business organization, to teach engineering at a university.

My father told me two things. He said, "I want you to know that my mental instability is not hereditary. You have nothing to fear. Secondly, it is not the result of any degeneration or dissipation. It's a question of biochemical balances in the body."

(Later, much later, I used to wonder whether the lithium in the blood was not more important than iron in the soul.)

Three years after my father told me I had nothing to fear, I was engulfed by the fear of madness. I was on a short holiday in Bombay, in August 1961. I became engaged to the girl I had known for six years and was generally happy when this fear came curving into my consciousness.

Krishnaji was in Paris. I was due to return to London in September. I wrote to him, and he welcomed me in his rooms in an apartment on the Left Bank near the Seine. His host was Carlo Suares and a friend, Léon De Vidas, was with him. He took me aside, listened to me carefully, and asked, "Do you exercise?"

The next day he told me, "Don't worry, you won't go mad."

The fear of madness has never returned.

Krishnamurti arranged for Monsieur De Vidas to invite me to stay with him for a few days in his house in the valley of the Dordogne.

I went to Tournon-d'Agenais, saw the frescoes of Lascaux, was a vegetarian in the heart of France, and in such close proximity to the great chateaus of Bordeaux and the Cognac district I didn't drink.

The fear of madness has never returned.

●

For over a decade thereafter I did not meet Krishnaji. I married, spent several years in Europe, and returned to India, all innocence gone.

The unintentional birth of my first child was a shock ("She comes into being as I anoint you with kisses"). I took a job.

I was in my thirties when I met Krishnaji again. He stayed at Sterling Apartments, where I lived in Bombay, and I used to walk with him every day on the racecourse. One evening, driving him back to the apartment, I started asking him about beauty and the relationship between men and women (we were alone in the car).

"When I was young," he said, "I lived in Paris for many months at a time. My brother was with me. I was well dressed, and I liked walking in the streets of Paris and going to good restaurants. And do you know, not one woman approached me or looked at me suggestively."

"I didn't know you went to restaurants," I said.

"Oh, occasionally," he replied. "My brother and I would engage in a long conversation with the headwaiter, in French of course, and order good wine. We then made some excuse about not feeling too well and ordered only vegetarian food. We gave the wine to the waiter."

And then he told me about a legendary Hollywood film star. He said they were in a house in Southern California, and she was with a world-famous musician.

"When she saw me, she stopped talking to him and embraced me, and later I went down to see her to her car, she put her arms around me again. I was taken aback, and she could see it."

On the plane from London to Los Angeles, Krishnamurti points out a mountain of ice that casts the shadow of a cathedral.

"Was she very beautiful?" I asked.

"No matter how beautiful..." he answered.

•

Many years later he said to me, "I am not against sex, it's natural when people are young. But now, Asit, see if you can look at sex differently."

"What do you mean by that?" I asked.

He said, "Don't suppress it. But don't give in to it. And don't run away from it."

"Then what do I do, if I don't suppress it, not turn away from it, nor give in to it?" I asked.

"Try it," he said, "you will see."

I did. I felt the most astonishing energy, a feeling of being totally alive. He said he could see the change in me. He left soon afterward for London. The feeling lasted a week, and I have never been able to recapture it.

•

We are in England in February. Krishnamurti and I are staying at Brockwood Park, the KFE school in Hampshire.

Krishnamurti is wearing a beret. It is cold outside, but he does not miss his walk. We return to the school and stand in the principal's office, where there is a huge picture of Krishnamurti taken in 1929. I photograph Krishnamurti in his beret standing next to his photograph. Krishnamurti is talking on the phone. He has never been good at it, and the conversation is brief.

The next day we take a direct flight to Los Angeles. This is the polar route, and there are vistas of whiteness. "No landmarks," I remark to Krishnaji, who is writing.

"Wait," he remarks. "In a few minutes, to your right, you will see an ice formation that casts a shadow like a cathedral."

The hostess, overhearing the conversation, says, "There are no landmarks or icebergs here."

"Wait," Krishnamurti persists. "You will see."

I load my camera and look out the window—just in time. Below us is a mountain of ice, and its shadow is that of a cathedral. I take some pictures as it recedes and look in wonder at Krishnaji. He has gone back to writing.

•

"When you have no psychological memory," he said, "your memory of physical things will be excellent. You know, I once spent a week blindfolded, I wanted to experiment, to find out what would happen. Of course, the other senses became much sharper."

•

Krishnaji and I were walking on the road leading out of the school at Rishi Valley. Krishnaji had turned to look at Rishi Konda, the hill that gives the valley its name. The sun had turned the sky red, miraculous as water becoming wine.

"That is what you must salute," he said.

Krishnaji looked and said once again, with hands folded and held high above and in front of his head, "That is what one salutes.

"Do you know," he said, "when I first saw the Parthenon, I fell to my knees...thank God nobody else was there."

We walked silently, and on returning stood outside the open assembly hall, where a great Indian singer was singing.

Krishnamurti stood in the darkness for some time, listening, and then went forward and sat quickly on the floor, where people had left their shoes and slippers. The audience inside was enraptured, and no one noticed Krishnamurti sitting quietly and listening to the singer singing to God, calling to him. Krishnaji listened for two hours, and then as he walked back to his room in total darkness, he said, "Do you know, all those songs were devotional, religious. None of the I-love-you-you-love-me nonsense of the West."

The singer continued long past midnight.

•

Krishnaji often asked me about computers and artificial intelligence. He saw it as a threat to the human mind; if the muscles of the mind were not exercised, the brain would deteriorate.

"Do you think that they will create a computer like the human mind?" he asked.

I replied, "The Japanese are attempting it, their so-called Fifth Generation Computer. They don't know what intelligence is, and that is the problem they are tackling. If they can find out what intelligence is, they feel they can create a machine to emulate human intelligence, to simulate thinking."

Krishnaji said, "So they are approaching intelligence through thought, thinking?"

"Yes," I said.

"Then it is totally wrong. Thought has nothing to do with intelligence, can never lead to it.

"And yet," he added, "people don't see the great challenge to the human mind, to consciousness, of the computer and genetic engineering and the new technologies. Shall we have a discussion, sir?"

And so we had many discussions, in many places, with many people, but that is in another entry, and besides the dialogue is not dead.

•

"If I knew the Buddha would be speaking here tomorrow, nothing in the world could stop me from going to listen to him. And I would follow him to the very end," Krishnaji said at lunchtime, in Arya Vihar, at Ojai.

A famous physicist from London and a well-known New York psychologist were present. There had evidently been discussion for many days about the validity of psychoanalysis. Krishnamurti said, "Analysis cannot lead to understanding or insight—observation and not analysis."

Before lunch the psychologist told Krishnamurti that he had not yet lost their "fight," it was only "the fifth round." Krishnamurti said quietly, "For me there is only one round."

Krishnamurti woke early in the morning, did over an hour of yogic exercises, dressed in a dark blue shirt and blue cardigan, went to the Oak Grove and spoke to three thousand people passionately, for an hour, from 11:30 A.M. to 12:30 P.M., on a beautiful cool day, then to Arya Vihar, lunched, and at the lunch table spoke intensely till 4:00 in the evening, went for a brisk walk for forty-five minutes at 5:00, and then returned to Pine Cottage.

It was Krishnamurti's eighty-fifth birthday.

•

We had just returned from a walk through the Grove, on the grounds of Brockwood Park, in England. It was the end of May,

and the woods were in blossom, the tall trees with flowers at their feet.

"Have you not noticed, sir," he said, "that when you enter a forest, the first time there is a strange atmosphere, as if nature, the trees, do not want you to enter. You hesitate, and say, 'It's alright,' and walk in quietly. The second day the resistance is less. And the third day it is gone."

I do not communicate with nature, and so this was something I had never discussed with Krishnamurti.

He said that he was doing his asanas in a small room in a cottage in India when he noticed a monkey watching him. "There were bars on the window, and the monkey stretched out his hand through the bars. I held his hand. It was the most extraordinary hand I have felt, rough on the palm, and very soft and silken on top. I held the monkey's hand for a few minutes, and then I saw that the monkey wanted to come in. I said, 'You can't come in. There is no room'. And after a while, still holding the monkey's hand, I said I had to continue my exercises, and the monkey went away."

He then told me stories about his encounters with animals—tigers and bears and rattlesnakes and even a lynx.

He said, "If you are sensitive, you are sensitive to everything. I cannot cut a rose, or any flower while it is alive. Do you look at flowers, trees, really look?"

"No," I replied.

"You miss a great deal if you don't," he continued. "One day I was walking in Benares, and we passed a grove of mango trees. My companion said that the trees hadn't borne fruit for many years, and they were to be cut down. 'Watch out!' I said to the trees. 'If you don't bear fruit you will be cut down!'"

"And what happened?" I asked.

"They bore fruit that year," he replied. "I am not saying it had anything to do with me."

•

Krishnaji and I left for London from Brockwood Park. Krishnamurti to a dentist—his tooth had been giving pain—and I on my way back to Bombay.

Krishnamurti came down the staircase at 9:45 A.M., looking extremely elegant.

The weather was good, the sun out, no clouds or signs of rain. I photographed Krishnamurti talking to Brockwood Park students at Petersfield station. We got a compartment to ourselves. Then Krishnamurti asked me to sit opposite him and said, leaning forward, "Is your brain alright?"

I was a little puzzled by the question. He then asked, "Is your brain free of conflict?"

I said, "No."

He said, "You know, any strong emotion is a shock to the brain. Anger, sudden anger, fear, a feeling of anxiety, all these upset the brain, and the brain gets affected."

I asked, "What about positive emotions?"

He said, "Like what?"

"Joy," I replied, "or ecstasy."

Krishnamurti smiled. "Oh, that happens rarely, doesn't it?"

He continued, "You must rest your brain between meetings, between appointments. When you are going to the office, on the way, look around you, don't keep thinking of what you are going to do or say at meetings. If you do, you have already formed a pattern, an expectation, based on your past experience of the person or the situation. That is the worst thing that can happen to the brain, constantly forming patterns, going round in grooves, thinking all the time. When I go to give a talk, my mind has no thought in it, so when I speak all the energy and alertness is there.

"You must exercise, and eat properly, and keep the brain healthy and functioning," Krishnamurti said, "otherwise it gets you later on. How old are you? Almost forty-one? That's not young."

•

As I grew older the effect his words had on me lasted for a shorter period. He used to watch me eat, and drink, and put on weight. He told me, "Be careful, sir. Your heart and your brain. Become slender and vital. Skip every seventh meal. Fill a tub with ice-cold water and take hip baths." He showed me stomach exercises, asked me to do them every day. His own stomach, which I touched, was hard and hollow. He told me his weight, at 51 kg., hadn't changed since his youth and that's why he could wear suits that were fifty years old. He taught me breathing exercises.

"Become slim and elegant," he said as he gave me his shirts and ties.

I talked to him about my frustrations, and how I would eat and drink through boredom and loneliness.

He told me, "If I had a wife, children, a job, I would still have two hours of leisure. And in those two hours I would go into fear, sorrow, desire, the process of thought. I would work at it, give it everything I've got, those hours would become my whole life."

He said, "You must have a certain amount of money. How much money do you need? Do you have it? If not, work for it, do your business really well, and make the money you need." I was quiet.

"Where would you like to live?" he asked. "What about California? Or India? If I did not have to live the way I do, I would live quietly in a village in India, such as Rishi Valley.

"The world is becoming a very dangerous place," he added, "what are you going to do? And you have children...."

"What would you do if you had children?" I asked.

"First of all," he continued, "think of them and not of yourself. Their lives and not yours. And don't use the word 'my' when you refer to them."

He talked about not being able to see something clearly if you are too close to it, a book becomes illegible if you hold it too close.

"If there is affection, you create an atmosphere where they feel secure, at home. I would talk to them about that. And then I would be silent with them, show them what it is to be quiet, silent. In that silence, their senses awaken, so that they look at a tree, listen to a bird, smell a flower."

"I would give them a good education, not spoil them," he continued. "Sir, there is no security. There is no protection. What can you do?"

And then he talked about protection. There are various occult societies, he said, and various practices. In some societies, at one stage you are initiated as a disciple to a master, and he makes an image of you, and every emotion, thought, and action of yours is reflected in that image, so that the master can watch over you. And at another stage two beings (he called them angels) are supposed to protect you.

"If you draw upon that power, however, it becomes weaker."

And then he added, "You must not do anything that is dangerous. You have to be very careful about this sort of thing."

"Why?" I asked.

"When one is protected, one has to be very watchful, for the bad as well as the good will be exaggerated," he answered.

As he said this he was very serious and a strange atmosphere filled the room.

He asked, "Can you feel it? If you talk about it you attract it..."

Then he got up and asked me to sit on a straight-backed chair. He walked a short distance, looked out of the window, jerked his hands as if shaking something off, and then came and stood behind me and with indescribable gentleness he placed his hands on my eyes, and then slowly drew his fingers over my head toward him. He did this several times, stopping occasionally to touch the spot between the eyes and at the top and back of the head and then the heart and finally, quietly, he laid his hands on my shoulders. As he walked away he said, "Sit quietly for a few minutes."

•

"You must never let anyone have power over you," he once told me, "and you must not have power over anyone else.

"When I left the Theosophical Society, and all the wealth and comfort surrounding me, Mrs. Besant said, 'What will happen to you? How will you live? How will you survive?'

"You understand, I had not been educated or trained for any profession. But here I am fifty years later...sometimes I wonder what I have done to deserve all this...

"Do the right thing, and the right things will happen to you," he said finally.

•

We were in Sterling Apartments in Bombay. He had noticed my lethargy and had taken me aside to talk to me.

"Do you love your children?" he asked. "Do you love anything? Do you love me?"

"Do you think I take you for granted?" I asked.

"Maybe that is it," he said. "Why don't you write to me, every day? You will see the difference it makes."

And then after a while he said, "If you spent some time with me I could change your life."

We were silent, and then he went in to have a bath. When he came out, just before lunch, he said to me, "I apologize for saying that."

"For saying what, sir?" I asked.

"That I could change your life."

•

Krishnaji ends a discourse to six thousand people in Bombay, and the energy that wells up in him during his talks is still emanating. The crowds surge around him. A policeman calls on them to move. Krishnamurti stops him by a sign and takes his hand and holds it. The policeman flings aside his baton and prostrates himself at Krishnamurti's feet. Krishnamurti lifts him up and, still holding his hand, enters the car. As the car moves, the policeman runs with it, refusing to let go of the hand.

We return and sit at the dinner table at Sterling Apartments.

"Why are you wasting your life?" he asks.

There is complete silence. He looks at me and says, "If you do not answer that question the moment it is asked, then you are wasting your life."

"And if I do answer immediately?"

"Oh, then you are an aristocrat."

•

He asked me, "Are you afraid of death?"

"I suppose so," I replied, "though at the moment there is no fear."

We had been talking about Yukio Mishima's commentary on *Hagakure*, a centuries'-old manual written for Samurais. I told Krishnaji that the book talked about always being ready for death, every morning to prepare for it. And that it was very important to be well dressed and even use makeup if necessary so that death would find one with rosy cheeks. To live with death all the time. And the Italians have a saying: "May death find you fully alive."

"Sir," I said, "twenty years ago I heard you say that one must enter the house of death with all one's senses fully alert, not when one is old and decrepit..."

"Yes," he replied. "For me the line dividing life and death has always been very thin. It would be so easy to live to be 150, but the body wears out with constant traveling and crowded airports and smoke-filled rooms, and so perhaps I shall live for another ten or fifteen years."

"What would happen if you were told that you were going to die tomorrow morning?" I asked.

He said, "Nothing. I would live exactly as before. The thought that death was so imminent wouldn't enter my mind again, and nothing would change."

•

Last summer I went to Switzerland to see Krishnamurti. We were sitting quietly together in Saanen. Krishnamurti was in his bathrobe, sitting straight on his bed, while I sat on a chair at the foot of the bed. Through the window you could see the snow on a high mountain, and nearer were the half-crescents of two other mountains, their points meeting to create the valley.

We had conversed for an hour or so, on bringing up children, education, meditation, death. It was a fragile conversation, touching profound matters lightly.

Suddenly he said, "If I were asked whether I had wasted my life, whether I am wasting it now, I would answer 'I do not know.'"

He was silent, and then he said, "I don't think so," and finally he added, "No."

"I might be wrong," he hesitated, and then said, "I ask nothing of the world. Perhaps that is the answer. I want nothing, from human beings or the Gods. Nothing, from anyone. If death came just now and said, 'You go this evening,' it would be alright."

He smiled. "You see, it's the same thing. I want nothing from this world or any other, and so I would go with death."

That evening I repeated the conversation as we sat in the car, before the walk through the woods above the stream in Gstaad.

"When I hear that it brings tears to my eyes."

And I remembered the Buddha, who said, "I obtained not the least thing from complete unexcelled awakening, and that is why it is complete unexcelled awakening."

•

POSTSCRIPT

I meet Krishnaji every year. Sometimes in Ojai, or New York, Saanen and Brockwood, and in Delhi, Rishi Valley, Madras, and Bombay. We go for walks and have long discussions in small groups, and sometimes just with each other. He stays in our apartment on his visits to Bombay.

As I write this I am forty-five years old. Krishnaji, in his ninetieth year, is twice my age. I finish writing and read a poem, Walt Whitman's *Leaves of Grass*:

...Who wishes to walk with me?

Will you speak before I am gone?
   Will you prove already too late?

And then a little later,

...You will hardly know who I am or what I mean,
But I shall be good health to you nevertheless,
And filter and fibre your blood.

Failing to fetch me at first keep encouraged,
Missing me one place search another,
I stop some where waiting for you.

INDIA

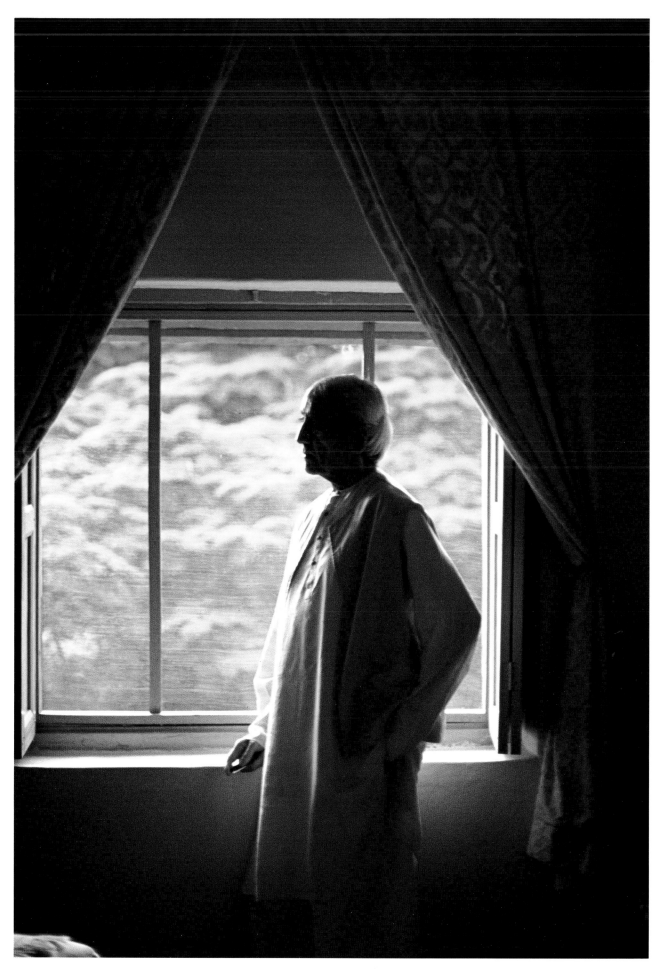

Krishnamurti in India at eighty-five.

Krishnamurti stays here in the corner room on the upper floor when he visits the school he founded in 1926 in Rishi Valley.

Rishi Valley is approximately twenty kilometers from Madanapalle, where Krishnamurti was born. Rishi means "sage." According to legend, for centuries rishis came to this valley to live, in meditation and the search for God.

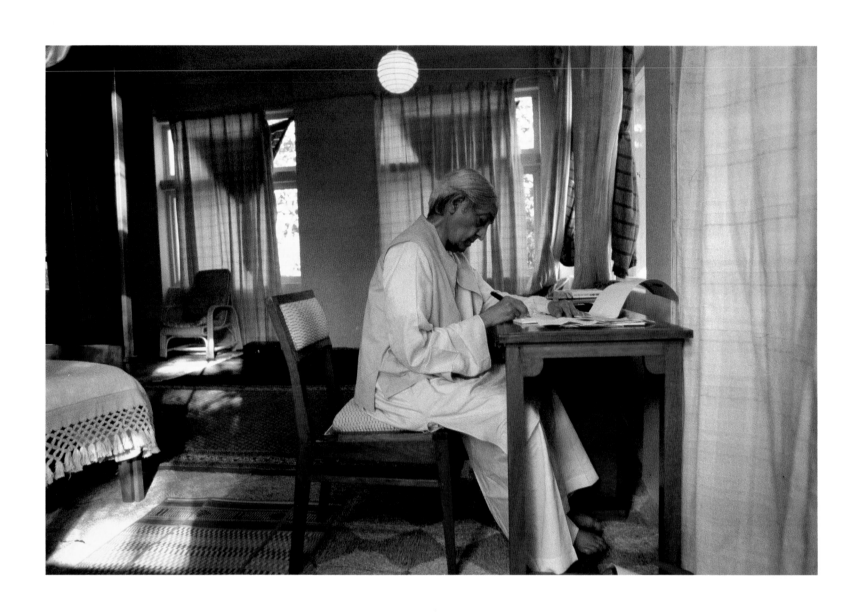

Krishnamurti in his room writing letters and consulting a dictionary.

Above: Krishnamurti prepares for his daily walk.
Right: After a talk with students, Krishnamurti puts on his sandals to walk back to his room.

Krishnamurti walks for as much as five kilometers—regardless of the weather. There is very little conversation. He has said that not a single thought touches his mind during these walks.

Krishnamurti walks on the grounds of the school with the late Mrs. Gandhi. The immense banyan tree in the background drew him to the site where he established the Rishi Valley School.

During the day Krishnamurti walks with an umbrella to protect him against the sun.
Below: Walking with Narayan, the principal of the school.

Krishnamurti points to a star at dusk.

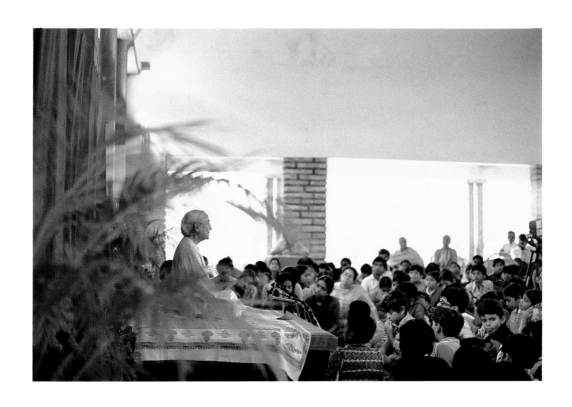

Above and opposite: Krishnamurti addresses students in the school's assembly hall.

Following: Krishnamurti speaks simply, articulately—his hands and face are vital yet gentle in their gestures.

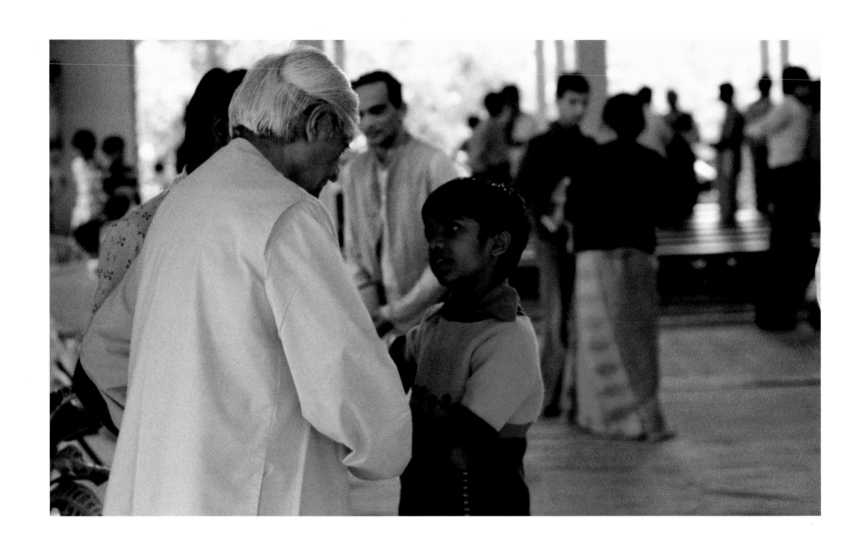

Above: After his talk to the students, he answers their questions.
Opposite: Krishnamurti sits in on musical programs and school plays.

Left: Krishnamurti meets with teachers at the school *(above)* and some members of his three foundations *(below)*.
Above: Krishnamurti with Nandini Mehta, Mary Zimbalist, Pama Patwardhan, and Pupul Jayakar.

Krishnamurti with Radha Burnier, president of the Theosophical Society.

Krishnamurti with Achuyt Patwardhan, one of his closest associates in India.

Above: Discussions with friends and associates take place at lunch. Facing the table are Krishnamurti, Alan Hooker, Mary Cadogan, and Dorothy Simmons. *Below:* Krishnamurti chanting Sanskrit verses with Narayan and Sunanda Patwardhan in Bombay.

In Madras, Krishnamurti stays in Vasant Vihar,
headquarters of the Krishnamurti Foundation of India (KFI).

Left: Walking on the beach at Adyar, where he was "discovered" in 1909. He was fourteen years old then, one among many, like the young boys playing in the background below.
Above: Krishnamurti walks with Rimpoche, a Tibetan monk.

Above: At a public talk in India.
On the podium, the silence of his presence creates order, no matter how large the crowd.
Opposite: As admirers press around after his talk, Krishnamurti reaches out and touches those who come to greet him.

The hands of Krishnamurti.

Left: Krishnamurti pauses during a discussion.
Above: Listening to Beethoven's Ninth Symphony after a public talk in Bombay.

CALIFORNIA

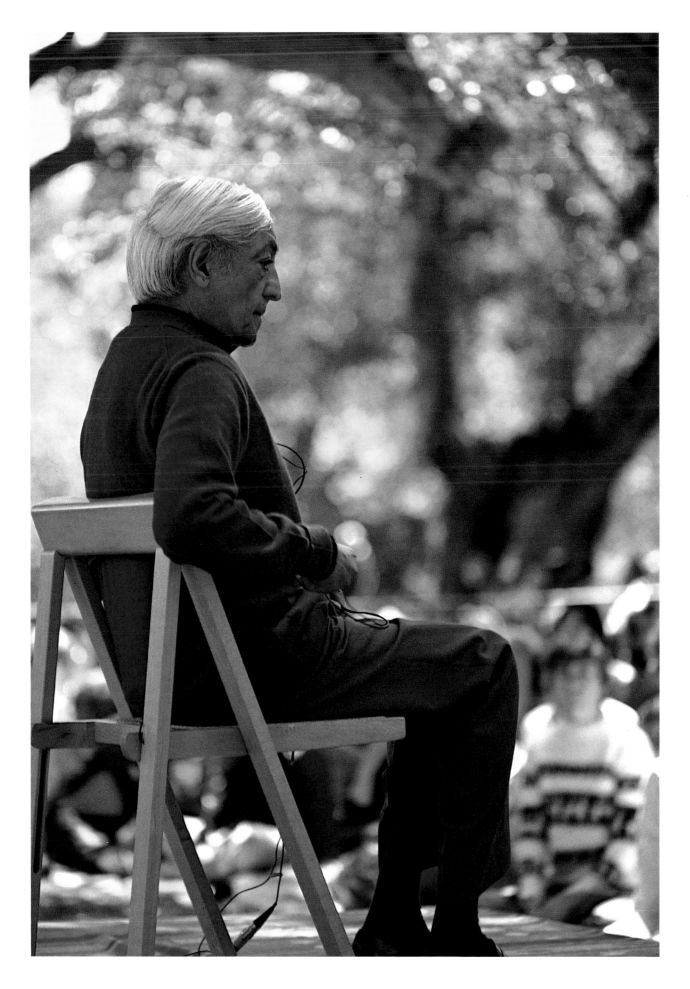

Krishnamurti at a public address in California. It is his eighty-fifth birthday.

The pepper tree at Pine Cottage, Ojai, California. Krishnamurti underwent his first "experiences" under this tree in 1922.

Krishnamurti has stayed here, at Pine Cottage, since 1922. Pine Cottage sits in the Ojai Valley.
At his school in Ojai, Krishnamurti talks to parents and staff about education and the significance of life.

Krishnamurti in the new addition to Pine Cottage.

Krishnamurti helps to prepare breakfast with Mary Zimbalist.
In the West, he helps clear the table, wash the dishes, clean the kitchen.

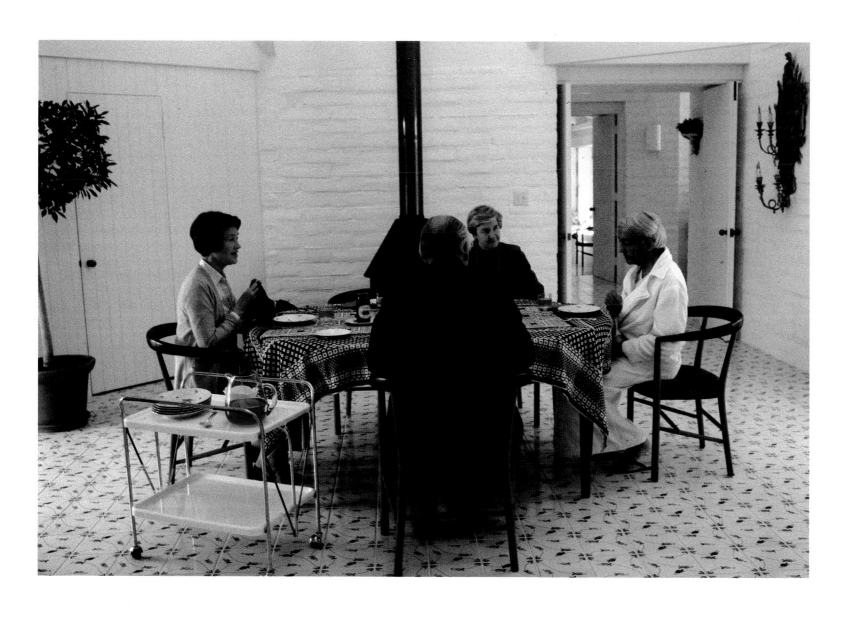

Mary Zimbalist and Erna and Theo Lilliefelt join Krishnamurti for breakfast at Pine Cottage.

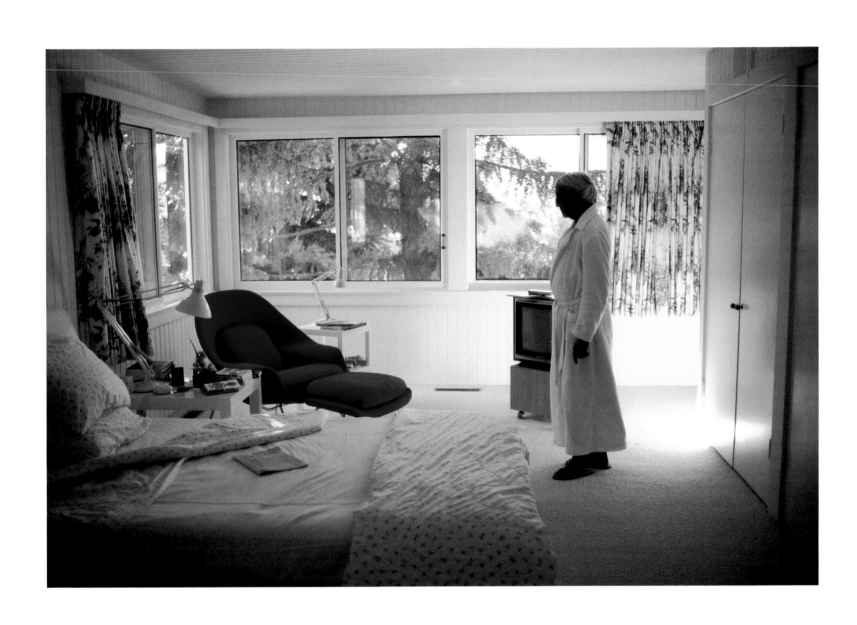

In his room at Pine Cottage.

Krishnamurti breakfasts alone in bed.

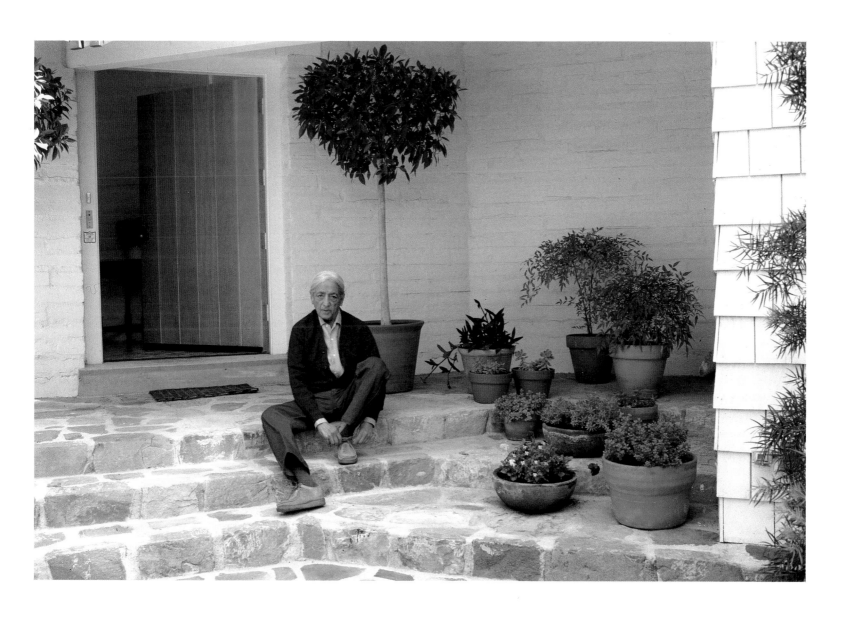

Krishnamurti prepares for a walk he will take in the hills surrounding the valley.

Left: On his walk with Mary Zimbalist and Theo Lilliefelt, Krishnamurti meets a jogger who offers him bee pollen. Krishnamurti is delighted. *Above and below:* Climbing over rocks in the valley.

Krishnamurti walks to Arya Vihar from Pine Cottage.

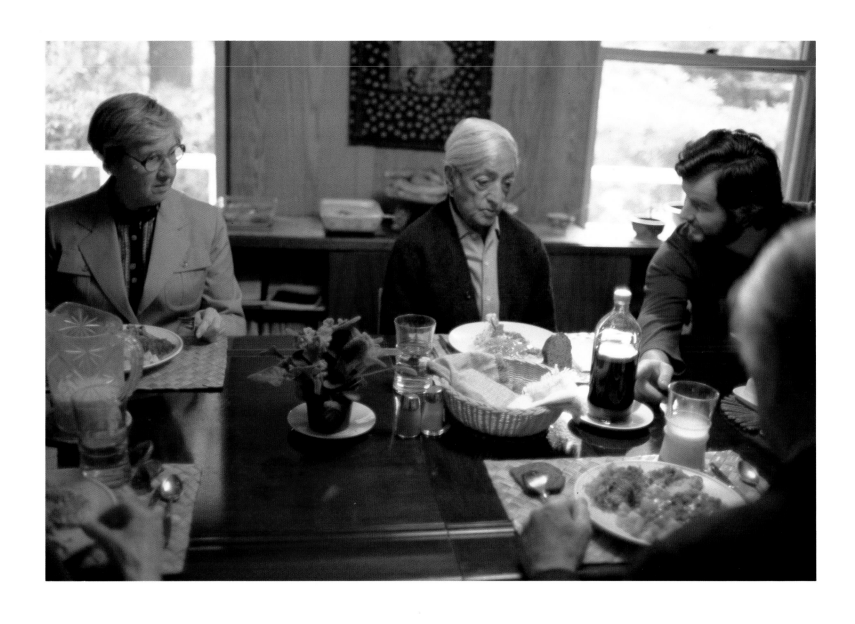

Krishnamurti lunches at Arya Vihar.
The cook, Michael Krohnen *(right)*, tells Krishnamurti the news of the world every day.

Krishnamurti always lets others precede him.

Krishnamurti loves to garden and does so energetically.

Krishnamurti and Mary Zimbalist at the Santa Barbara airport, where they have come to pick up a friend.

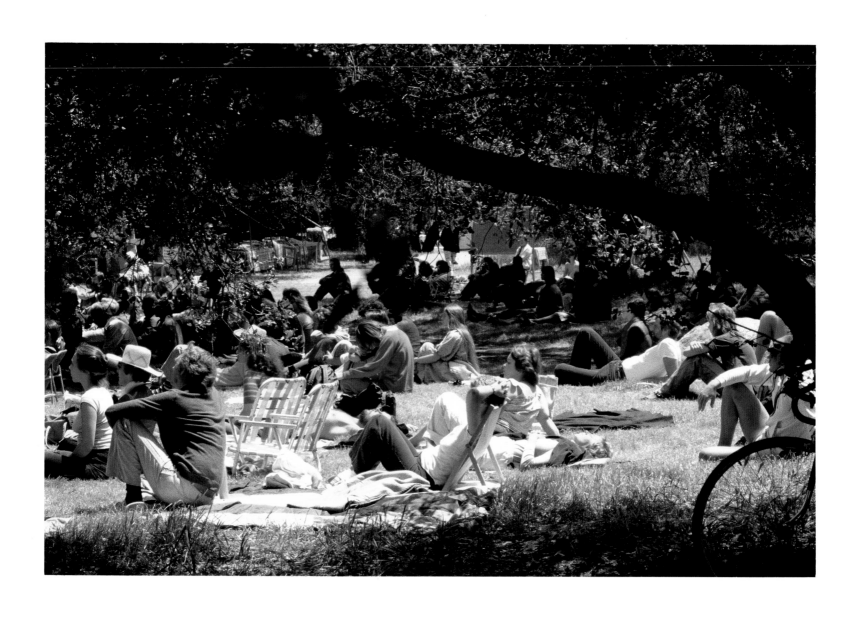

Above: A crowd assembles to hear Krishnamurti speak at the Oak Grove.
Right: On the podium before Krishnamurti's talk commences, Alan Kishbaugh attaches a microphone to him.
It is May 11, 1980. On this day Krishnamurti is eighty-five years old.

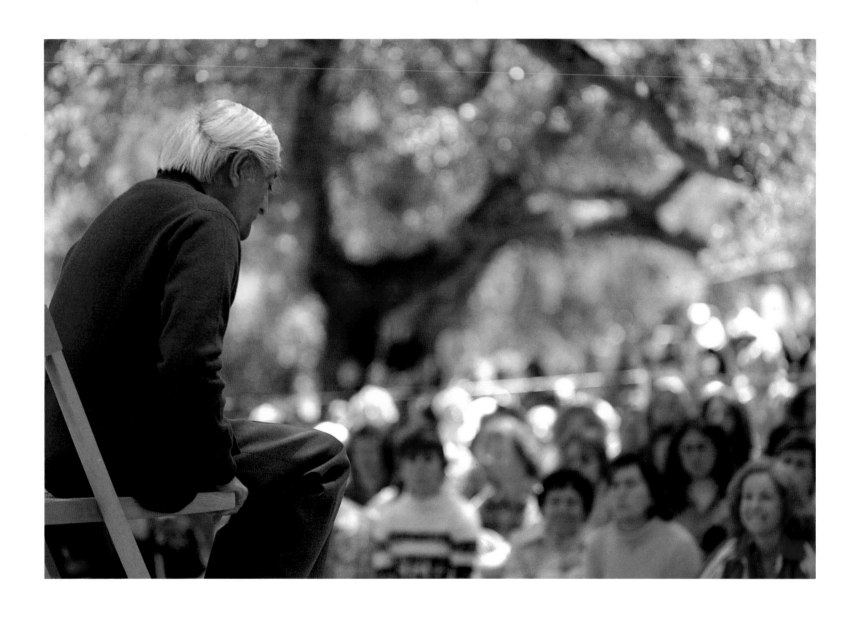

As he sits in silence on the platform, Krishnamurti's presence reaches out and draws his listeners close to him.
Then he starts to speak.

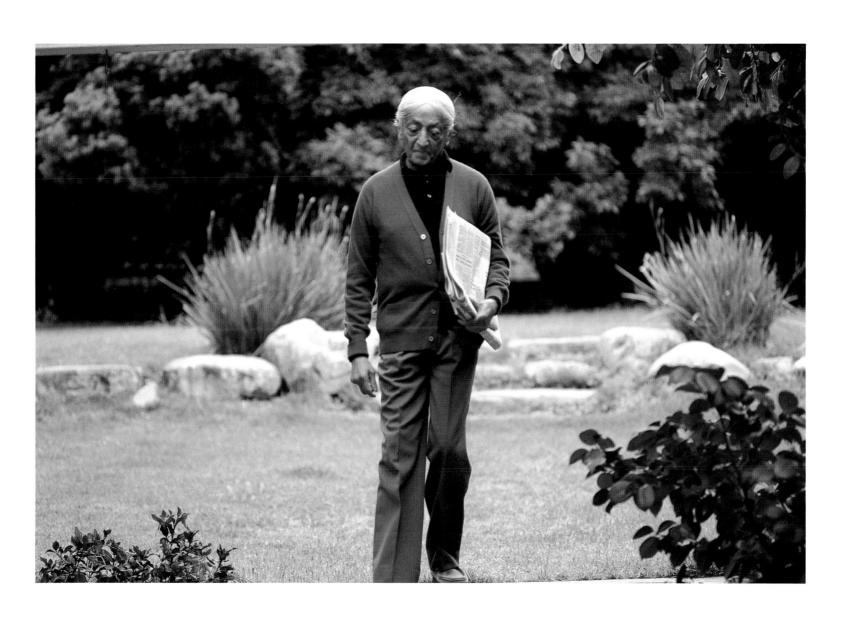

Returning to Arya Vihar after his talk.

ENGLAND

Krishnamurti on the grounds of his school at Brockwood Park.

The Krishnamurti Foundation of England (KFE) school of Brockwood Park, Hampshire, England.
The Brockwood Park School was founded in 1969 with money a donor had originally intended for Krishnamurti's personal use. "You are seventy years old," the donor had said to Krishnamurti, "I'll buy you a house in the south of France, provide you with a cook, a maid, a car, and so on. You can stay there the rest of your life."
"I'm not interested," Krishnamurti replied. "If you really mean to donate this money, could we use it to start a school?"

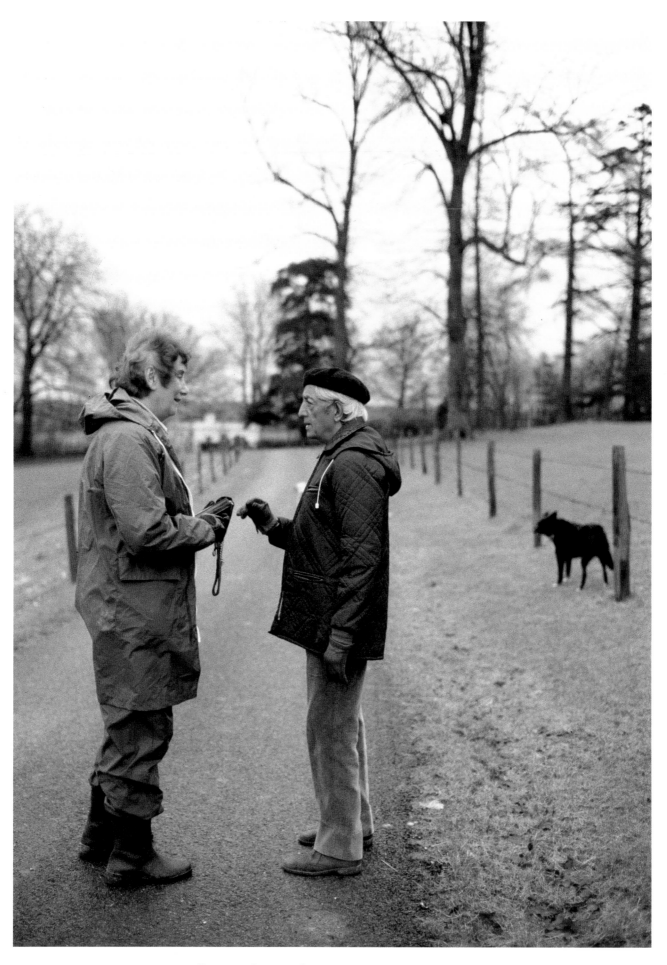

Above: Walking with Dorothy Simmons, principal of the school.
Right: Krishnamurti in the principal's office with Doris Pratt, standing next to a portrait of his taken in 1929.

Most people half his age cannot keep up with him—here, near Brockwood Park.

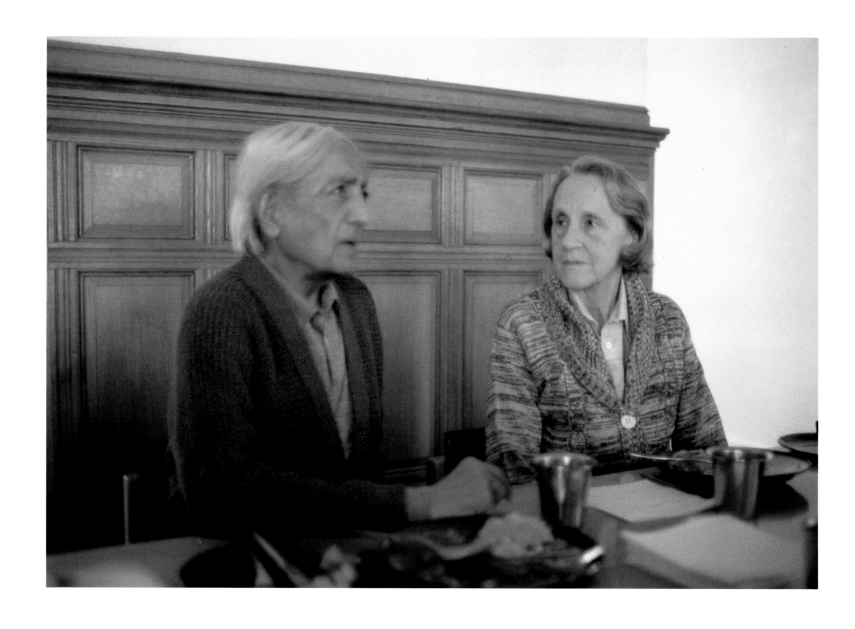

Krishnamurti lunches with Mary Lutyens, a close friend he has known for seventy-five years and whose family looked after him while he was a young man living in England. Lutyens' father was the architect of New Delhi, her grandfather a viceroy of India, while she herself has written a two-volume biography on the life of Krishnamurti.

Krishnamurti and Dr. David Böhm, a physicist, friend, and associate, during a discussion at Brockwood Park.

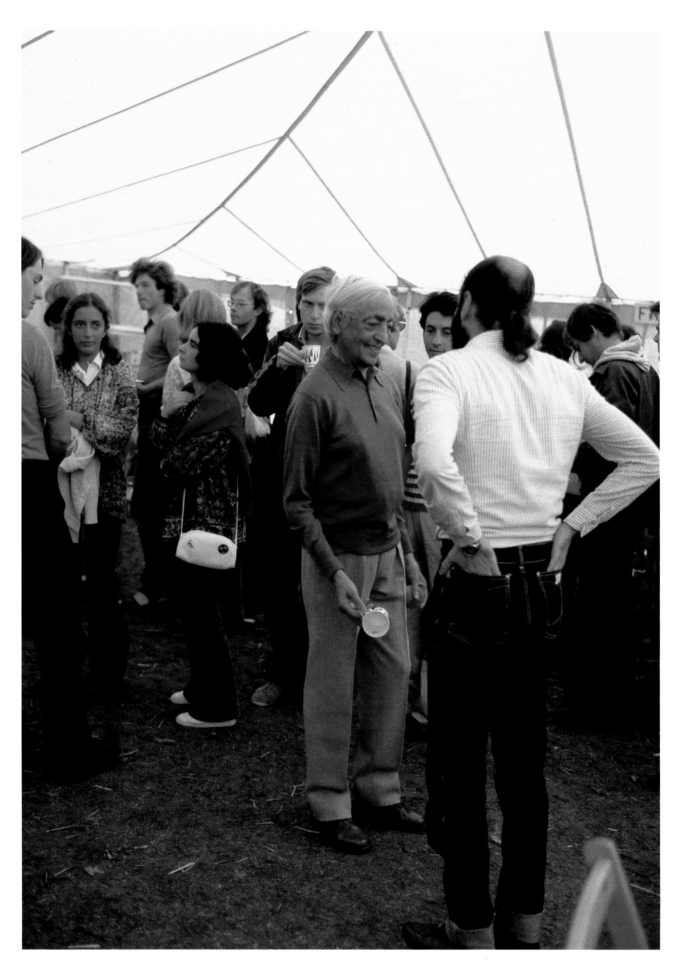

Above and opposite bottom: After a talk, Krishnamurti returns to a tent where lunch is served and he mixes with the audience.
Opposite top: The crowd gathers for his talk.

Krishnamurti bidding goodbye to the students and faculty as he prepares to leave Brockwood Park for California.

Krishnamurti chats with students from the school as they all wait for the train to London.

On the train to London.

Above and opposite: On a plane from London. Krishnamurti reads, writes, watches a movie, eats, sleeps, and takes his walk up and down the aisle of the plane on a long flight.
Below: Krishnamurti looks at thrillers and other light reading before catching his flight.

SWITZERLAND

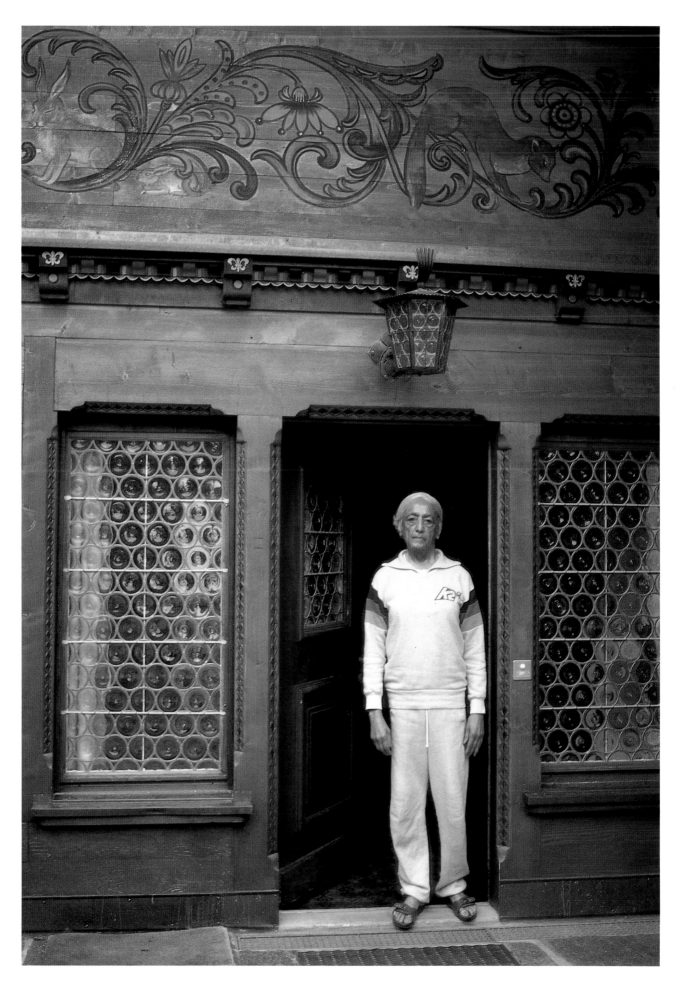

Krishnamurti in front of Chalet Tannegg in Gstaad.

Gstaad, Switzerland. Krishnamurti has been coming here since 1959.
During his stay each year, he gives public talks in Saanen, four miles away.

In Gstaad, Krishnamurti stays at Chalet Tannegg, a rented chalet.

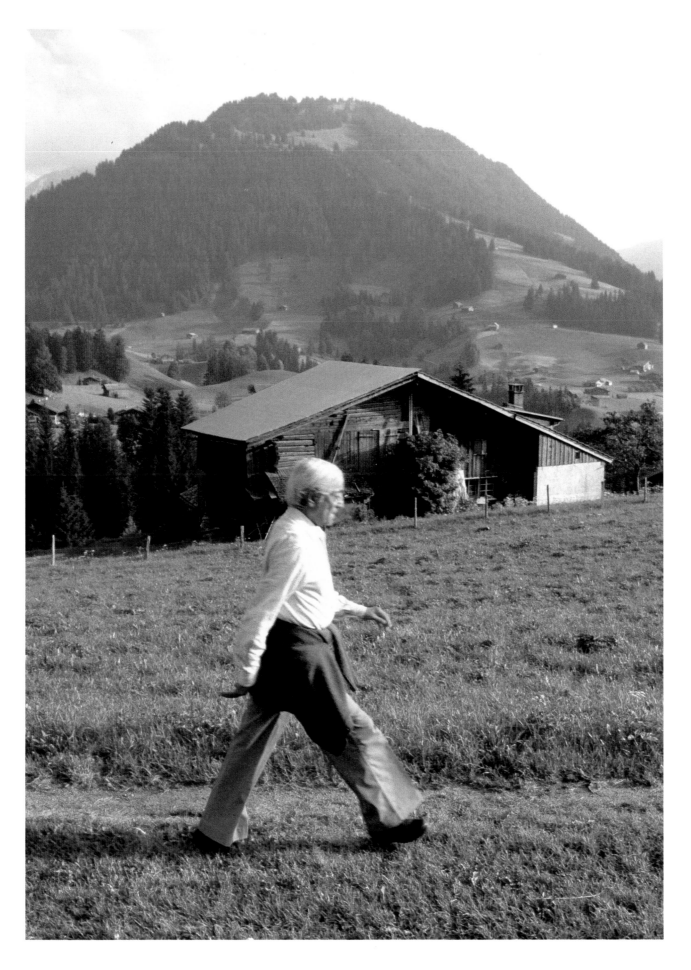

Krishnamurti's stride is long and vigorous.
Here he walks in the woods above a stream, his favorite place for a walk in Gstaad.

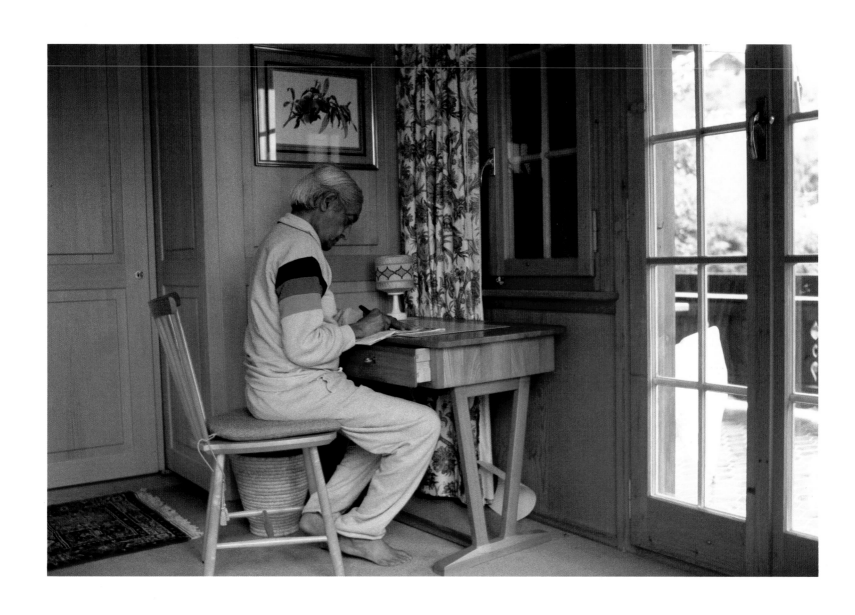

Krishnamurti writing, after his morning exercises.

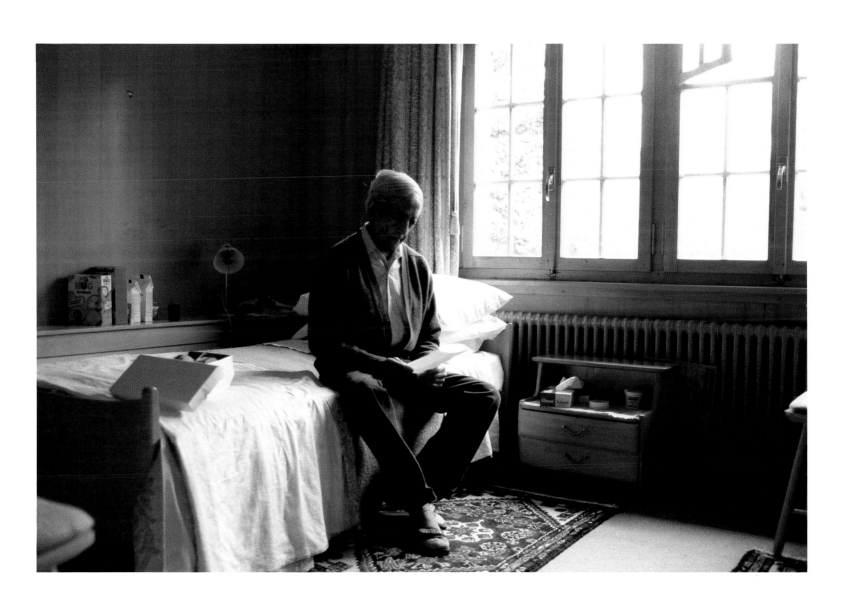

In his room, Krishnamurti reads a letter before lunch.

Krishnamurti with Alain Naudé, Minakshi Chandmal, Mary Zimbalist, and Dr. Parchure.

Krishnamurti helps carry visitors' luggage outside the chalet.

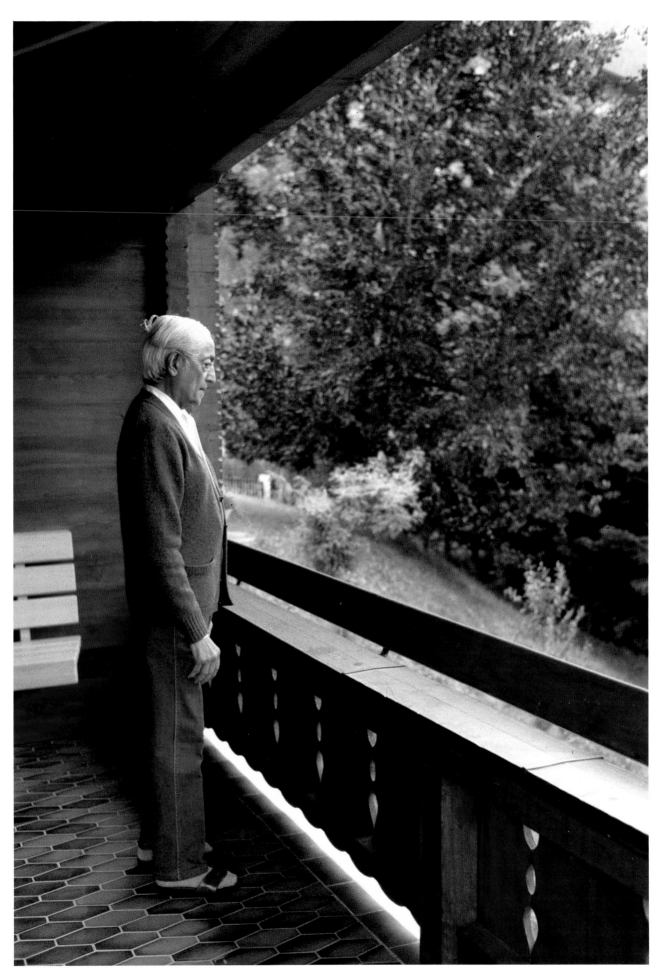

Krishnamurti on the balcony at Chalet Tannegg.

THE LAST WALK

I see him now, stepping out of the portals of Vasant Vihar in Madras, walking with his nephew Narayan, two proud Brahmins, one ninety the other sixty, looking decades younger, dressed in the clothes of ancient India, striding toward the platform under the lit tree, awaited by thousands.

He climbs slowly onto the cloth-covered platform, and sits in meditation, alone, as if on the lonely high mountain where a small stream is perpetually being born as the Ganga.

Then he speaks.

"Something entered me," he tells me later that evening. "Something happened to me."

He speaks of the birth and beginning of all energy, the perception of the path into the source of all creation. At the end of an hour, he sits in silence. A child walks up with a flower. He turns and smiles and takes the white champak flower.

The child smiles. The sermon ends with the silence and the smile.

He has said it is the last talk.

•

Among the lasting images is that of my aunts and cousins weeping silently in the second row of chairs, while my nieces and daughters sit upon the ground, the sad stories of the death of kings on their faces. It is the evening of the 4th day of January, 1986. The body has six more weeks to die.

•

On the evening before the last talk, on impulse, my eighteen-year-old daughter Clea flies in from Singapore to see him. She has not met him since she was thirteen years old, a student at Rishi Valley. We go to see him in the morning. As we enter his room he sits up to talk to her. We talk about molecular biology, and genetics, and what will happen if the computer and these technologies meet and combine and grow. What will happen to the human brain?

And then he turns to her and says, "You are going to Cambridge. The professors there are very clever, Nobel prize winners, all knowing a great deal. They know much more than you do. They are the authorities. They will say, 'We will teach, we will speak and you will listen.' What will you do? How will you study with men who dictate to you their findings, and tell you to learn what they teach? With what quality of mind will you meet such minds?"

An extraordinary energy emanates from him.

Just then Parameshwar, the cook, enters with breakfast. He puts the tray of idli and ghee on the bed. Krishnaji offers us some of the food and asks if we want tea or coffee. When Parameshwar leaves I repeat his last question to him. He does not seem to understand. My daughter tells me not to press it. Later she said, "He is two different people, the teacher and the man." She felt he had no memory of the conversation we had just prior to Parameshwar entering the room.

But that evening, halfway during the last talk, he smiles at her sitting on the ground in front of him, and talks about genetics and the computer coming together, and its impact on the human brain. "What will happen to you then?" he asks the audience.

•

On the days that follow he meets his friends and associates from the Krishnamurti Foundation in India, sometimes alone, sometimes in a group.

He speaks of many things, of schools and study centers and silence. Toward the end of the last gathering he says, "Be absolutely alert, and make no effort."

I ask if these are his last words to us and he smiles.

•

Though he is weak and losing weight, and has his meals in bed, he goes for a walk every evening. Every evening it is the same walk.

He drives from Vasant Vihar to Adyar, through the grounds of the Theosophical Society, until he reaches Radha Burnier's house on the sea. She is the president of the society, an office she won in election against her aunt Rukmini Devi Arundale.

He walks on the beach where he was "discovered," found and adopted and initiated by the sea at Adyar, seventy-five years ago, when Halley's comet last entered the orbit which would carry it toward the sun.

•

When he was thirty-four, he had walked out of the Theosophical Society, and rejected everything that had been built for him, renounced everything that had been given to him, with the words, "Truth is a pathless land . . . if you follow someone you cease to follow truth." He had renounced more than any man since the Buddha ("Renunciation is intoxication") and yet Radha was a friend, and perhaps something at the end drew him to his beginning.

On one of those last evenings he stopped by at Rukmini Devi Arundale's house, and they spoke together. She was a great Theosophist like her husband, and Krishnaji had come to a parting of ways with them, so when they met it was after half a century. Rukmini too had six more weeks to live.

●

He has been talking about his death openly and freely. He tells me one evening, "Dr. Deutsch will examine me a week after I reach California. If he says no more travel, no more talks, then it's all over. The body will die in four weeks."

Then he asks, "What are you going to do with your life, sir? If you have touched the other, and are not anchored in it, you will go to pieces."

●

At 5:30 in the evening of the tenth day of January he goes for his last walk. He is to leave for California at midnight.

As usual, he walks through the garden of Radha's house, through the walled gate, opening and closing it carefully, and turns right along the beach. There are boats and boys on the beach, darkened by the sea and sky. As he strides along the shore he is silent.

He holds Radha's hand as he walks, reaches out and touches Nandini Mehta on the shoulder, resting his hand on her as he walks, then turns around, and walks past Radha's house to the other end of the beach, where the broken bridge ends, and the Adyar river becomes the Bay of Bengal (less than two months later, his ashes are to be scattered here). He stands silently, looking at sea and sky. He is completely alone. Then he turns and faces each direction, and becomes the silence, the sea and the sky.

He turns and starts walking toward Radha's house. He lets everyone precede him. His hair streams behind him, like a comet's trail.

We reach the house and he lets everyone pass through the gate. He stands aside. When he is alone he once again faces each direction for a few moments. He sees the sand, the sea, and the sky, and that is his farewell.

●

That night at midnight, he comes down the circular stairs from his room on the first floor, and his old associates are standing in a half circle to say goodbye. He greets each one of them and at the last, Pupul Jayakar, whom he asks jauntily,

"How do I look Pupul?" and she replies, "Very young."

I meet him on the plane. He is wearing a gray Huntsman jacket, dark gray trousers, and a maroon scarf. The plane takes off just after midnight, and Krishnaji leaves India for the last time, not far from the place where he was born, just after midnight, ninety years ago.

●

At 4 A.M. on January 24, I phoned Dr. Parchure in Ojai from Singapore. He had just returned from the hospital, and told me that Krishnaji was in intensive care. Though Krishnaji had always said that he did not want to go to the hospital when he was dying, they had no choice. Krishnaji was in great pain. The doctor said that he could not treat him without knowing the cause, and the tests could only be done in the hospital. He was admitted to Santa Paula Memorial Hospital on January 22. I read later in the doctor's report that an ultrasound test had earlier revealed a three-centimeter mass in the right lobe of the liver and within a week it had grown to eight-centimeters. A needle biopsy was unsuccessfully attempted, and then serologies (involving the application of monoclonal antibodies) revealed cancer of the pancreas which had spread to the liver. After consultation with a top oncologist it was felt that no further diagnostic tests were necessary. Krishnaji was told that there was no chance of recovery. He asked for and was given all the facts. He was discharged on January 30, since he wanted to leave the hospital and return to Pine Cottage at Ojai.

●

My aunt Pupul Jayakar, her daughter Radhika Herzberger, who is the Director of Rishi Valley School, and I travel together from Delhi via Amsterdam to Los Angeles, reaching Ojai on the evening of January 31. Professor Krishna, the head of the Rajghat educational institutions, left a day earlier, and Mahesh Saxena, the secretary of the Foundation in India is to come as soon as he gets a passport and a visa.

Pupul is traveling Business Class, while we are on excursion tickets. Radhi and I carry a silver urn with us. There is a vacant seat next to us, and the urn rests on it. We buy the Amsterdam–L.A.–Amsterdam tickets at Schipol airport. Since it is an excursion fare, we have to specify the return date. Radhi and I look at each other, knowing fully the implications of giving a date. Finally, we decide on February 16.

On this flight to Los Angeles too there is a vacant seat next to us, and Radhi looks after the empty urn while I sleep.

The next morning, on February 1, Pupul, Radhi and I go to see the Krishnaji at Pine Cottage. He is lying in bed, and though he greets each one of us individually for a few moments, he hardly recognizes us. His attention span is a few seconds. His eyes close after each greeting. I stand aside in a

Krishnamurti with his close associates and biographers, Mary Lutyens (left) in London; Pupul Jayakar (right) in Bombay, 1980

state of deep shock. Was this the man I had walked with at Adyar three weeks earlier?

●

The next day he is much better and is able to talk for a few minutes at a time to many of his close associates. Mary Lutyens, the daughter of the architect of New Delhi, and other members of the English Trust have also flown in, and all of us lunch together every day at Arya Vihar, a few hundred yards from Pine Cottage.

And so the days pass. Some see him, some don't. Some leave, some remain. He speaks to some, he is silent with others.

He asks me, "What are you anchored in, sir?"

After a moment's hesitation, I answer, "In you, sir."

"I'm gone," he replies.

●

The doctors are unable to say how long the body will live. It is unpredictable, it could be a matter of a few weeks, or a few days. Not a few months.

One afternoon he asks to be taken outside the cottage. He is carried out and sits silently under the pepper tree where he had his first experience of enlightenment in 1922. He asks to be left alone.

Then he says, "Take me a little further so I can see the hills." This is done. He again asks to be left alone. There are groves of orange trees around him, with many oranges and the fragrance of white blossoms.

He bows his head slowly to the sky and the hills.

●

On Wednesday, February 12, Halley's comet has circled the sun, and is on its journey away from the sun. Pupul phones that Krishnaji has been hemorrhaging. A violent storm comes from the Pacific Ocean. The Ojai Valley and the roads leading up to it are lashed with unprecedented rain for two days. Mud slides block the roads leading to the valley, there is danger of total isolation at the far end of the valley where Pine Cottage is situated. Some homes are evacuated, and television crews are seen in Ojai filming the deluge.

The storm passes on Friday, February 14.

I speak to Krishnaji that day. I say, "All your life you have helped others, you have been concerned about others. You have helped me all my life. May I ask you, if it is at all possible, can I help you? I am not talking about the body, that is being looked after, I am asking how can I, how can we, help you?"

He listens with his eyes closed. He opens them, smiles, and says very seriously, "Don't let anyone spoil the teaching."

Then he closes his eyes again.

He later calls to see me and asks me about my visit to Silicon Valley. What is the latest in computers? Are the Russians spying? Are the Japanese catching up? He listens very intently and I am (and perhaps he's too) momentarily back in Rishi Valley, and he is the Krishnaji I know, engaging in dialogue and discussion.

●

On February 16, he is in great pain. I hear his pain when I go to Pine Cottage at eleven in the morning. When there is respite from the pain I go into his room and stand at the foot of his bed. He recognizes me and holds out his right hand, and beckons me to come nearer. He holds my hand and his grip is strong. He asks, "Are you all right? Are you comfortable? Are you all right?" I say, "Yes," and he closes his eyes.

I leave the room.

●

That night I cannot sleep though I am exhausted. At eleven o'clock the atmosphere becomes frightening in my room. The fear persists. I want to be with someone.

I force myself to sleep. An hour later I am woken up by my hostess. "Krishnaji has just died." I am disoriented and for a moment do not know where I am and what she is saying. She repeats, "Krishnaji has died."

●

I jump out of bed, dress quickly, and just then Mark Lee comes to pick me up. Mark, a very close associate, has specifically been entrusted by Krishnaji to bathe his body after death ("I have always been a very clean man, wrap it in cloth. I have no nationality") and to cremate his body without any ritual, rite, or ceremony whatsoever.

Mark asks me for a dark tie. I give him a black silk Charvet tie which Krishnaji had given me years earlier. I grab a pair of socks, and see the initials JK on them. He has always given his material possessions (mainly clothes) to others. In the few weeks before his death he had given away virtually all his clothes, both Indian and Western, to some members of the three foundations.

When we arrive fifteen minutes later at Pine Cottage, Krishnaji is already bathed and wrapped in a simple white cloth, with a pink and gray blanket up to his chest. His face is unlined, peaceful, beautiful, with a faint smile.

Dr. Deutsch had been with him when he died at ten minutes past midnight of the 16th (or 0:10 A.M. on February 17). He had not been in any pain since about 8:30 P.M. when he had fallen into a deep sleep.

I cannot help kneeling at his feet when I see his body (I have never in my life been able to prostrate myself before anything or anybody, but this time it is an inevitable and natural movement). There are two or three others alternately keeping vigil in the room. Lawrence Durrell's *The Alexandria Quartet* is by his bedside, and *Palgrave's Golden Treasury*, the *Oxford Book of English Verse*, Italo Calvino's stories, *The Berlitz Dictionary of Italian*, Alphonse Daudet's stories, and Gustave Doré. Books in English, Italian, and French. His Patek Phillipe timepiece with an ancient Greek coin on a chain on the table.

I make calls to India to break the news.

●

The undertakers are to take the body at eight in the morning. A few minutes before that I pluck a white camellia from a bush on the porch outside the room where Krishnaji's body

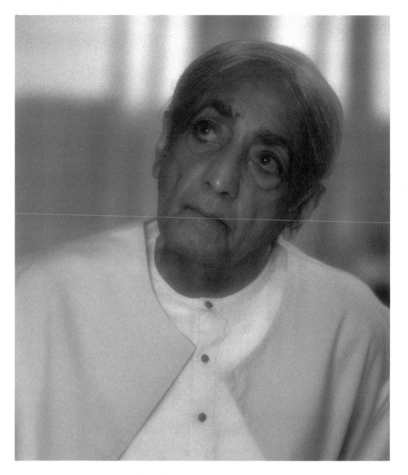

Krishnamurti in 1980

lies. I also pick up a camellia which lay on the floor, because he had once asked me while walking, thirty years ago, "Have you ever picked up a fallen flower from a dark lane?" and had shown me the flower he had just picked up.

I put the fresh flower at his feet. I do not think it is a rite or ritual. The flower is from all of us. I go out to put the flower in a glass of water and keep it on a table in the room.

I return to find the face wrapped. The face that has taken centuries to refine, and who knows what otherness to make divine, that face would not be seen again.

The undertakers come. The body is put in a brown cardboard box which is then closed. It is 8:10 A.M. The body is carried through the porch on a trolley to the waiting station wagon under the pepper tree. It is a sunless sky.

We watch in silence. A great flock of hundreds of gray geese flies east in a perfect *V* formation over the body in the station wagon under the pepper tree. There are three cars which follow the station wagon for almost an hour to the Ivy Lawn Cemetery at Ventura. The crematorium is beside the Pacific Ocean.

The blue steel door of the cremation oven is raised. We examine it to see that it is clean, that there are no other ashes in it. Then the box with the body is slid into the oven, the door closes and the flames are started. It is 9:10 A.M.

At 11:10 A.M. the attendant fills the silver urn we had brought from India with the ashes. Carrying the urn we step outside. At that very instant, the sun comes out and floods the urn and the lawns of the cemetery.

•

Mark drives Mahesh and me back to Ojai. I am carrying the urn in my lap. It is warm. It is like that for an hour, before the warmth slowly gives out, as we reach Ojai.

The ashes are divided into three urns—one for America, one for England, and one for India. "Scatter the ashes. Let no one tread on them. Grow trees over them. Let them be anonymous."

Ojai Valley awoke to the news that morning, and the news spreads gently. There are no crowds, not even groups of people, only the silent separate mourning of deeply affected human beings.

•

Mahesh and I fly from L.A. to Delhi on the evening of the 19th. We change planes at Amsterdam, reaching Delhi on the morning of the 21st. On both flights, there is a seat vacant next to Mahesh where he keeps the urn.

Pupul receives the ashes at the foot of the plane. She places a rose on the urn, takes it from us gently, and drives straight to her house at 11 Safdarjung Road, where Krishnaji stayed when in New Delhi. When she steps out of the car there is a sudden and unexpected downpour, a hailstorm which drenches my aunts and cousins as they carry the urn to the foot of a great tree on the lawn, where Krishnaji once gave a discourse. The urn is surrounded by flowers. The lawn is white with hailstones for a moment. Just then the sun rises. Standing there I feel the sacred. "If there are only five people who will listen, who will live, who have their faces turned to eternity, it will be sufficient."

•

I cannot write anymore. I have been writing since five in the morning—for six hours—writing on the dining table in Sterling Apartments, where he used to sit and eat—there was so much laughter. I sit on the chair opposite his. He once told me, when a great friend of his had died, "When someone dies, there are one or two persons he or she may want to see. They will only come back to a house where there is no violence, where there is love."

Time does not pass, only you and I do.

This text originally appeared in Bombay *magazine, March 7, 1986.*

Krishnamurti at Adyar beach in Madras, during his last walk, January 10, 1986

THE CORE OF KRISHNAMURTI'S TEACHINGS

The core of Krishnamurti's teachings are contained in the statement he made in 1929 when he said: "Truth is a pathless land." Man cannot come to it through any organization, through any creed, through any dogma, priest, or ritual, not through any philosophic knowledge or psychological technique. He has to find it through the mirror of relationship, through the understanding of the contents of his own mind, through observation and not through intellectual analysis or introspective dissection. Man has built in himself images as a fence of security—religious, political, personal. These manifest as symbols, ideas, beliefs. The burden of these images dominates man's thinking, his relationships, and his daily life. These images are the causes of our problems for they divide man from man. His perception of life is shaped by the concepts already established in his mind. The content of his consciousness is his entire existence. This content is common to all humanity. The individuality is the name, the form, and the superficial culture he acquires from tradition and environment. The uniqueness of man does not lie in the superficial but in complete freedom from the content of his consciousness, which is common to all mankind. So he is not an individual.

Freedom is not a reaction; freedom is not choice. It is a man's pretense that because he has choice he is free. Freedom is pure observation without direction, without fear of punishment and reward. Freedom is without motive; freedom is not at the end of the evolution of man but lies in the first step of his existence. In observation one begins to discover the lack of freedom. Freedom is found in the choiceless awareness of our daily existence and activity.

Thought is time. Thought is born of experience and knowledge, which are inseparable from time and the past. Time is the psychological enemy of man. Our action is based on knowledge and therefore time, so man is always a slave to the past. Thought is ever-limited and so we live in constant conflict and struggle. There is no psychological evolution.

When man becomes aware of the movement of his own thoughts he will see the division between the thinker and the thought, the observer and the observed, the experiencer and the experience. He will discover that this division is an illusion. Then only is there pure observation which is insight without any shadow of the past or of time. This timeless insight brings about a deep radical mutation in the mind.

Total negation is the essence of the positive. When there is negation of all those things that thought has brought about psychologically, only then is there love, which is compassion and intelligence.

This statement was originally written by Krishnamurti himself on October 21, 1980, for "Krishnamurti: The Years of Fulfillment," by Mary Lutyens, the second volume of his biography, published by John Murray Ltd., in 1983. Copyright © Mary Lutyens. On re-reading it, Krishnamurti added a few sentences to this text.

Krishnamurti's last walk, Adyar beach, Madras, January 10, 1986